TRANSFORMATIVE TESTIMONIES

The wonder of God in the modern world

Edited by John Hemming-Clark

© Searchline Publishing 2023
and the individual contributors

First edition 2023

ISBN: 978 1 897864 69 2

British Library Cataloguing in Publication Data available.

Published by Searchline Publishing, Searchline House
Holbrook Lane, Chislehurst, Kent, BR7 6PE, UK

Tel: +44 (0)20 8468 7945

www.johnhemmingclark.com/transformativetestimonies

Printed in England by www.catfordprint.co.uk

Compiled and edited from contributions,
by John Hemming-Clark.

Contents

Introduction

The hand on your clock of life has just one revolution. It starts at the top and goes all the way round to twelve and that's it, your life on earth is over.

What have you done so far with your life on earth?

Where are you on that clock? The truth is, you don't know.

The time to sort your life out is now. Those nagging questions, not the ones about what you're having for dinner, for example, but the big questions such as, "Why am I here?" and "What's it all about?"

Do you have any answers?

This book is not an easy read. You may be very offended by it. You may find that it attacks beliefs that you hold dear. There are some contributors in this book who have experienced between them desperate situations that have involved different faiths, drugs, alcohol, New Age and other spiritualism, Satanism, shamans, witch doctors, pornography, abuse, war, physical and mental illness, death, apartheid, self-harming, cults, prison and divorce. Others have just been a little lost.

Sounds fun doesn't it? The truth is, many of our lives are a bit of a mess but there are answers to the big questions. If you're plumbing the depths of despair, the chances are some of the contributors have fallen further. It may be that you're feeling fine but just occasionally wonder.

This book is for you, whoever you are and wherever you are in life.

Every story in this book is a first-hand account of hope. You will experience a whole range of emotions reading these true stories and they will change you in some way, I'm sure of that.

So if you're ready - time is ticking therefore read on...before the hand on that clock gets all the way round.

John Hemming-Clark

Imagine

When I was a baby I was completely dependent on others. I wasn't consciously storing up memories but I was gathering experiences: Sights, smells, sounds, tastes, touches.

When I was a very young child I began talking to people. They started to speak sentences to me that I understood. Some of the things I said and did I remembered for many years. I started school. School was fun. I soaked up so much stuff that I thought my brain would burst!

By the time I was a teenager I had made a few friends. I had learnt how to ride a bike. I knew that a few things I said and did were wrong. I had to say "Sorry" quite a bit. I kissed someone.

By the time I left school I was ready for anything that came my way. I went off to university and gained a degree but also had three fabulous years in a strange city with new people that would become friends for life.

Assured, keen and independent I threw myself into the world of work. In my spare time I discovered things that were ever-so-slightly hidden and took full advantage of them. Fortunately I was never caught and they were just a phase I was going through. I learnt to drive a car. I was out most evenings.

Later on in my twenties I met the most wonderful person in the world. I feel desperately and deeply in love. I married. I bought a flat. It was tiny but it was a start.

In my thirties I had children. I had no money so I stayed in most evenings. I would sit chatting and I often recalled all that I had been up to when I was younger. I read a bit and occasionally looked at the TV. I had an allotment. Then I bought a house. I watched my children grow up.

I blinked and I had reached retirement age. I stopped the nine to five but kept on with a little bit of work now and again. I did some volunteering.

In my eighties I was seriously ill but I survived. My family was a great comfort to me at that time. I stopped doing sport and took up jigsaw puzzles.

In my nineties I began to lose my faculties and I so had to be looked after, firstly part time and then all the time. I became interdependent. I don't remember much after that.

During my life, from time to time, I would gaze up at the stars and wonder, sometimes in awe but often just with a slight yawn.

I am no longer in the world. How I desperately wish, more than you can ever imagine, that somebody had told me whilst I was alive on earth of the wonder of God in the modern world. Maybe they had but I didn't listen. Maybe if I had listened I would have believed. If I had believed it would have saved my life.

A bit of this story is me as it probably is with you. However, the following stories are all true. They are first-hand, real experiences and they may just change your life.

Amy's story

From a traumatic childhood and miserable young adulthood Amy contacted a friend from years ago who helped to give her hope. She then began to have supernatural dreams in which Jesus appeared to her.

I'm a single mum to a lovely young girl. I was raised as a Muslim. My dad was practicing and was fairly strict, my mum not so much, she was a little bit more relaxed.

When I was growing up as a teenager it was quite a troubled time. There was a lot of trauma and pain. As I got older I felt very alone and I couldn't really talk to anyone. My dad died when I was twenty-four and I continued to go through a really difficult time. I was in an abusive relationship and I found myself very isolated and alone. There were plenty of traumatic events that led up to and through that period and so it wasn't the easiest time growing up.

I believed in something; I believed in God but that was as far as it went. I just believed that there was a god but I didn't know how or what, I had just kind of left it at that and did a lot of things in my own strength. I thought that I sort of had my life back in order by that point having got out of this relationship but I wasn't really content. I got married and had a child and so thought, "This is it!" However the marriage broke down. Even though I had a child there was still always something missing but I couldn't put my finger on it. It wasn't until my marriage had broken down that I thought, "I can't believe that I'm going through all this again," and once more I found myself lost and alone and in despair. One evening whilst I was feeling miserable I was scrolling through social media. I came

3

across a friend that I had known years ago, probably ten to fifteen years ago. When I had known her she wasn't a Christian, she was very much into stuff like New Age. She was playing the guitar and was singing a worship song. I thought, "How strange." Anyway I reached out to her, mainly because she was a single parent with three children. I said to her, "This may seem a bit odd but how do you manage from day to day?" We spoke on FaceTime and she was really great. At the end of our conversation she prayed for me. I didn't understand about the Holy Spirit or God or anything so I just accepted it; I was desperate. I did feel peace but I didn't know what it was at that time.

I started watching some sermons and I found them inspiring, positive and helping to lift me. They were beginning to give me hope. However, at the end of each one when the preacher would say, "If you don't know Jesus and you want to know Jesus and invite him into your heart say the salvation prayer*." Then they would say the prayer. I would always stop the videos at that point because I refused to do it. I couldn't bring myself to say that Jesus is the Son of God and I believe in Him; I just couldn't do it. However I kept on and on listening to them, then one night I just said, "Okay, fine! If you are who you say you are and you're going to give me all this hope and this promise then just show me, show me who the real god is because I don't know and I'm confused and I'm lost and I'm broken." So I said the salvation prayer without actually knowing what I was doing but then something happened.

I started having dreams with Bible verses being given to me. I would look them up and they were always so relevant to what I was going through; they were always so comforting. That was the main way He spoke to me initially when I first

4

came to Christ. He spoke to me through dreams, giving me scripture verses. These dreams were always very different dreams to my normal dreams. I knew that these dreams were from God because they would be so etched on my brain.

I then had two dreams with Jesus actually coming to me in them. It's an experience I can't really explain. I knew it was Him although I couldn't see his face as it was so bright. It was too overwhelming to look but it was Jesus.

It's been a real whirlwind of a journey to know that a god loves you that much, and it's very personal. It's not just He loves you, yeah, he loves you and that's it. No, He loves YOU that much that even if you were the last person on Earth or the only person on Earth He would still have died for you.

*Dear Lord Jesus, I know that I am a sinner, and I ask for Your forgiveness. I believe You died for my sins and rose from the dead. I turn from my sins and invite You to come into my heart and life. I want to trust and follow You as my Lord and Saviour. Amen

Bernard's story

Bernard was so caught up in war in Sudan that he came to the conclusion that life wasn't worth living. As he was thinking about how he could take his life he heard a song coming from a chapel and life was never the same again.

Until I was seven years old I lived peacefully with my family in southern Sudan. However that all changed in 1964 when the First Sudanese Civil War reached our village. I fled to Uganda with my sister's family. We began our twenty-two mile journey on foot but because the main road was infested with soldiers we had to access the border another way.

When we crossed the river into Uganda my brother-in-law put me behind his head, my baby niece was over his shoulder and his right hand dragged my sister through the raging waters. We ended up in Gulu but the rest of my family settled at Elegu near the border and so we were separated.

Back then in the 1960s refugees didn't have tents. We had to construct our own hut. The Ugandan authorities gave us machetes for cutting wood and hoes for digging land but that was it; that was all that we had. We made a mud hut to live in. It had a grass thatched roof.

When I reached twelve years old I discovered that my father had died. The authorities wanted to relocate refugees nearer the border and so went about moving them. My dad suffered from severe asthma and was unable to leave, nevertheless soldiers still bundled him into a lorry. He died from an asthma attack.

When I was fifteen years old the Addis Ababa Peace Agreement was signed. This signalled hope that we would be able to return home. Mum decided it was time to leave.

My brothers returned to Sudan first so that they could construct huts for our family. My job was to look after the family's possessions while mum sought transport for repatriation. However it was so chaotic and slow that mum decided it would be quicker to walk the twenty-two miles across the border alone.

As she crossed the river into Sudan the military that were hiding in the bush caught up with her. They probably raped her and left her for dead so that she would not tell her story to the world. My siblings in Sudan thought that my mum was with me whilst I thought she was with them. Two weeks later we discovered the burnt remains of mum hidden under a bush.

I tried to pick up the pieces of my life. I got a free place at secondary school but, with over five hundred students, I felt lost in the crowd.

With no proper home, I boarded at school during weekends and holidays.

Every Sunday I would sit under the same mango tree in the school grounds wondering why my life had been wrecked by war and poverty. I felt lonely.

Life wasn't worth living.

One Sunday, when I was wondering how to take my life, I heard a song coming out from the nearby chapel.

When I heard "What a friend we have in Jesus," I felt that I was being called. I left my tree, walked in and sang with the rest of the students. That was the beginning of my new life.

Life was never the same again!

The chaplain who was leading the service worked for ACROSS - a development agency in Sudan co-founded by Christian aviation charity Mission Aviation Fellowship (MAF).

These people gave me the hope and direction that I so desperately needed.

My new faith gave me internal peace, but society around me was crumbling into chaos. The Second Sudanese War erupted in 1983.

Aged twenty-nine I had my new wife and baby daughter to think about so we fled to safety in Nairobi. With commercial flights closed at Juba Airport the only way out was with MAF.

In 1990 ACROSS offered me a job in Nairobi where I boarded many MAF flights to support Sudan's development. During this period I completed a Masters degree in publishing at Scotland's Stirling University. I also trained as an Anglican priest.

Unfortunately the Kenyan government didn't extend my visa, so once again my family faced an uncertain future.

Australian missionaries offered to sponsor us so a new life in Sydney awaited. We migrated in 2000 and joined a

Sudanese community. Many of us struggled with Australian culture. As their church leader I supported them but I underestimated the toll it would have on my health. Domestic violence was common among the community and I was in and out of police stations with various youth problems.

By 2004 it was getting too much. I slipped into depression and had a breakdown. My wife left me because I was like a vegetable. It took me a year to become human again.

When the Second Sudanese Civil War eventually ended in 2005 after twenty-two years, I wanted to leave Sydney and return to Africa. Once again God answered prayer.

Aged fifty-four I finally returned home. South Sudan had gained independence in 2011 but peace didn't last long. The South Sudanese Civil War marred my country from 2013 to 2020.

Today Juba (the capital of South Sudan) is very different from what I remember. When I left it was just a village.

Before the Second Sudanese Civil War security was not a problem. Poor as it was we could still walk around at night and nobody would worry us but now I struggle. I know things could be done better because of my experience in Scotland and Australia.

Today, at sixty-six years old, I find solace in Grace Community Church that I founded in 2011. We serve missionaries from all over the world as they endeavour to rebuild South Sudan.

I know there are things that only God can change in my country. I dream that the war will cease and that political leaders will put their people's interests first.

I thank God for Grace Community Church. It has become a chaplaincy for many MAF staff and other Christian organisations. I am very appreciative of the selflessness of these people.

My encouragement to them is to soldier on. They are not alone. May God who has sent them here continue to look after them and their families. As a product of missionary work myself, I just want to give thanks to God for MAF, which has been in my life for a very long time.

Carole's story

Having parted company with God, medical issues brought Carole back to the church years later. God intervened to give her a longer life.

As a child going to church on a Sunday was a regular occurrence. However, in my late teens, following various traumas, I parted company with God, church and everything connected with it for the next twenty-five to thirty years.

Then I became ill with a cardiac problem that doctors battled to resolve. On one particular occasion I was in hospital for a month. Being in a side room I did not see the other patients but God had made my presence known to another lady who was a committed Christian. This lady, after various abortive attempts, gained access to my room whereupon she told me how she had been directed by God to tell me that he loved me and wanted me to serve him.

Wow, initially I was sceptical but the more this lady talked to me, the more I began to trust what she said.

Following my discharge I decided to return to God and church. I attended a couple of churches but felt unwelcome; I walked in and walked out. Then I found the church where I was welcomed and supported and have been there for over twenty years.

To support God's love for me further, a few years ago I needed surgery. I returned from the theatre at around 9.45pm to find my poor mother still at my bedside. I sent her home and told her to ring and let me know she was home safely.

During that period of waiting the Charge Nurse from another ward wanted to pop in to see me. The staff said, "No," as they had settled me. Sometime after that my mother 'phoned the ward to let me know that she was home. The staff decided to come and tell me. They found me having gone navy blue and not breathing. I had had a respiratory arrest. Clearly I was resuscitated!

I firmly believe that God directed the actions of the staff. He was not ready for me to die that night and had other plans for me.

Charles' story

One man's remark that a teenage Charles overheard led to Jesus without him being freaked out.

When I was a child I used to go on holiday with my neighbours. There were four of us youngsters and I was the only boy.

When I was thirteen we stayed in a guest house in Wales. One evening I was listening to a group of adults talking in the sitting room. One of them said that the only thing you need in order to get Jesus into your life and to live in eternity with him is to say sorry for all your sins and to ask him in. "He will come," this man said. I don't know who this man was and he will never know what an impact he has had on my life. Just one sentence in a conversation and I was changed forever that night.

As the only boy and as I was now thirteen years old I was told I would have to have a bedroom by myself. I was therefore confined to a room that was obviously the overflow or spare. It had a bed but that was about it. It was in the middle of the building so had no external window. As I lay in bed in the complete dark I was frightened. "Invite Jesus into my life?" It felt so compelling yet I was totally freaked out by what would happen if I asked him. What could happen? I reasoned that asking him was probably a good thing and so the chances were I wasn't going to be abducted by aliens or come to any serious harm. I shut my eyes and prayed for Jesus to come into my life. But before I did I asked, "Please God, I don't know what's going to happen but please don't freak me out."

Although all was black in front of my eyes as it usually mostly is when they are closed, especially in a darkened room, suddenly that blackness lit up and in its place was bright yellow light, brighter than I had ever seen before and have seen since, but I wasn't blinded. And in the middle of all this light there was a large cross, a large empty cross. A sense of indescribably beautiful peace came over me and I knew then that Jesus is as real as anything else I had experienced and would ever experience. Fifty years on and I recall that experience as clearly as if it were happening to me now; it was as real as the fact that I am now sitting at a table writing about it.

I kept my eyes scrunched shut the whole of that night praying, "Please don't freak me out any more." In the morning when I awoke and thought that it was safe to open my eyes I looked at the wall at the end of the bed. Up high there was an internal window and beyond it light from part of the kitchen was coming through. The window was comprised of four panes of glass and they were separated by a wooden frame in the shape of a cross. I hadn't noticed it before but then I knew that God had truly answered my prayer: he had come into my life but had done it in such a way as not to freak me out.

My life since has been spent following Him and he now regularly freaks me out, not with aliens but with awe.

Charmaine's story

From apartheid in South Africa and a teenage ambivalence toward God that saw Charmaine walk away from Him, a priest's praying for her after a medical issue manifested itself gave her the light of hope in her tunnel of despair followed by God's presence in her kitchen.

Hindsight is a great teacher. When I look back on my life I see that it is the times when I wandered furthest away from my heavenly Father that he drew closest to me.

I grew up in South Africa during the apartheid years. For readers too young to remember, apartheid was a political system which segregated people into four main race groups: whites, "coloured" (multi-racial), Indians and blacks. Each race group had to live in its own area, attend its own schools and marry within that group. It was illegal to have sexual relations or to marry someone from a different race group! Worse, unequal educational funding and reservation of higher-paid jobs for white people kept them rich, everyone else poor. As an Indian I was disadvantaged but nowhere near as much as the black people of South Africa.

Writing about this now makes me sad, but apartheid was a very real and normal part of my childhood. I grew up in an exclusively Indian suburb, went to an exclusively Indian school and, as a child, had very little contact with people from other race groups. I recall seeing "Whites only" signs on restaurant windows and park-benches but didn't question them. I just accepted that the white people I saw on shopping trips to the city centre were somehow better than me. I remember going to a beautiful deserted beach one summer with my family. My sister and I remarked in the changing-room how nice and clean it was. When we got back to my parents we found two police officers with them explaining that we couldn't picnic there because it was reserved for "coloured" people. We had to pack up and move off down to the Indian beach which had poorer facilities.

The shocking corollary is that I viewed black people as somehow less than me. A childhood incident might explain this better. My parents had bought a new fridge and it was delivered by two men, one black, the other white. Usually manual labour like carrying heavy furniture was a black person's job, but in this case the white man was there to connect the fridge to the mains. It makes me furious now but I recall us children running in from the garden, barefoot and dusty, to gawp at the white man in our kitchen. It was a searing hot day, over thirty degrees Celsius, so my dad offered them a drink. The white man got his in one of our best glasses while the black man got his in an enamel cup which we reserved for passing black vendors. So you see, racism was stamped into me from an early age and when my eyes were opened to this it shook my faith in everything I had always taken for granted, including the goodness of God.

Despite the shadow of apartheid, I had a wonderful childhood in a loving Christian family, the youngest of three daughters. Before I was born my parents had hoped I would be a boy and had even named me Terence; they must have been disappointed but never showed it. My parents lived out their faith in ways which formed a deep impression on me. I recall evenings with us kids gathered around my parents' bed, taking turns to read from my dad's leather-bound black Bible and then to pray together. My dad once

16

told me that the Bible had cost twenty-one guineas, a costly sum which he had scrimped and saved from his very first earnings. This taught me about the preciousness of God's Word. Our Sundays revolved around church, and some of my earliest memories were of helping my mum tie her saree while my dad was trying to get us into our dresses, lacy socks and shoes. We had to hurry so we wouldn't miss the bus. Public transport in Indian areas was minimal so missing the bus would have meant missing out on church, and I can't recall that ever happening!

More than just church and family prayers, Christianity was a way of life. Despite being poor and living in a very basic council home, my parents were hugely hospitable and would welcome unannounced visitors warmly, sharing with them whatever we had. My mum is a dab hand at turning the simplest ingredients into a delicious curry, so friends and family were always dropping in. And my parents went out of their way to help people, even total strangers. A lady whose car broke down near our house was welcomed in and offered tea and biscuits while she waited for her mechanic to arrive. I have often wondered what she thought sitting in that simple, shabby room. Perhaps she read the text of the picture-frame hanging on the wall: *Christ is the head of this home* and sniffed the aroma of Christ mixed with the smell of curry. Perhaps seeds of faith were sown that day. Eternity will tell.

As a child I loved Jesus. I loved listening to stories about Jesus which my mum read to me from an old book of Bible stories we had. I was particularly drawn to a drawing of Jesus in that book. In the picture a blond Jesus was sitting with white children, one upon his knee. I looked at that picture and longed to be the one sitting on Jesus' knee, longed to have him smile and talk to me too. My mum assured me that Jesus loved me *even though* I wasn't white. That picture and her words created in me a suspicion that Jesus loved white people more; perhaps that conclusion was inescapable in the world I lived in.

My teenage years at secondary school were marked by the birth pangs of political dissent. Television had finally been allowed into South African homes in the 1970s and, despite being heavily censored, international television shows were opening our collective eyes to the fact that as far as race relations were concerned things were very different elsewhere. We could see black and white people playing sport together, shaking hands even. The Cosby show was revolutionary! At school history lessons were used to vent against apartheid.

I began to see that we had all been fed lies, and I wondered about how Jesus fitted into all this. As far as I knew there had never been a sermon on the injustices of apartheid in the Pentecostal church I had grown up in. And I couldn't blame them for this. Draconian internal security laws outlawed freedom of speech. But I was still angry that my parents were so blind to all this, so meek and submissive. Couldn't they see that their lives were so hard because they had not been given better opportunities? Couldn't they see that apartheid had trapped them in poverty? One day I visited a museum in the city centre. The museum exhibits explained an important moment in South African history, the Battle of Blood River, when the Dutch settlers defeated a much larger Zulu army. The settlers believed that God had given them victory and empowered them to rule over all other races. Of course I'd learnt all that in school, but seeing the exhibits - life-size wax figures and replicas of Dutch ox-wagons - made it much more real in my mind. The God who gave the Dutch settlers victory was the same God my parents and I worshipped. How could this be? Did God love white people more? Were they also his chosen race? Was that why God was allowing apartheid to happen? So many questions. No answers. And so began my wandering away from the Lord.

Looking back, it wasn't a dramatic decision to stop loving Jesus, just a slow and gradual drifting away. I never stopped believing that Jesus is God, I just didn't want Jesus to be lord of my life. I wanted to be the boss of my life. So when I was at uni. I stopped going to church, choosing instead to work part-time at a large supermarket. I started hanging out with a group of friends who drank heavily and did dope. By the sheer grace of God I didn't lose my focus on my studies. Several friends dropped out of uni. but I graduated from law school and won a scholarship to Cambridge. Then I got hired by a London law firm where I met my husband. Life was very busy. I had a comfortable home, fun friends and a happy marriage; I had come a long way from the little council house in South Africa. But I was so blind I honestly believed I had achieved all this on my own; I didn't see or acknowledge how much God had blessed me. My life could so easily have turned out differently but for his saving grace. I'm ashamed to say that I was like the kid at Christmas who gets the super-cool toy and spends all day playing with it and ignoring the person who gave it. I was happy to take all God's gifts but not to acknowledge him as the source of the gifts, never say thank you. Basically I treated God with contempt.

There were a few times when I felt a pang of guilt and thought of returning to God, but then I thought of all the sins I'd committed in the past. I could almost imagine God wagging his finger at me in judgment. Perhaps one day I'll clean my life up, start being "good" again and then I could return to God, I thought. Just not now.

So the years passed. I had two children and began attending church with them, mainly because I wanted my children to grow up in the church. I also quit my job, did a master's degree in creative writing and started to write a novel. It took about two years but when it was finished I had a mental breakdown, the main symptom of which was anxiety and preoccupation with negative thoughts. For example, I would drive to the local Tesco and not be able to get out of the car because I was just sobbing from anxiety. Other times I would drop my kids at school and be too anxious to go home. I was diagnosed with a debilitating mental disorder and prescribed medication but it made me so sick I stopped taking it. I also began cognitive behavioural therapy but that didn't help either. I had grown up thinking that I could always rely on my mind, but now my mind was disordered, and it was terrifying. Have you ever had a dream where something terrible is happening, and you open your mouth to shout for help but no sound comes out, no matter how hard you try? You can see the terrible thing happening but you're powerless to prevent it. That's how helpless I felt; but even in my helplessness, I still refused to turn to God. I was still stubborn and proud.

I recall my mum saying to me one day, "I'm praying for you." I snapped back angrily, "You might as well stop praying because your God doesn't answer prayer." Praise God she didn't listen to me. She just kept praying, trusting that the Lord would answer.

God often answers prayer in ways we don't expect, and He answered my mum's prayers by allowing me to contract a skin infection, a horrible rash over my face which couldn't be diagnosed. I consulted a dermatologist who had no clue what it was and what to prescribe. Skin swabs came back unresolved. Worse I was told that the infection had gone too deep and that I'd always be scarred. It was literally the straw which broke the camel's back. I'd had enough. One morning I called the vicar of the local church my husband and I had recently started attending and asked him to come to pray for me. To my surprise he dropped whatever was on his schedule and came that afternoon. As he prayed, I started weeping and couldn't stop. I had no idea what had come over me. It felt as if a stone in me, something rock hard in my chest, was dissolving. For the first time in a long time, I could see the light of hope in my tunnel of despair. But God had only just begun....

A week later, I was alone in my kitchen, listening to a CD someone from church had lent me. It was Matt Redman's "Blessed Be Your Name." The lyrics reminded me of a verse I'd heard over thirty years ago, as a child, from the book of Job, "Though he slay me, yet will I hope in him." I still recall the tone of our family pastor saying that verse; it had made an indelible impression on my mind.

And then I felt something I can only describe as the presence of God. I couldn't see him, but I just knew God was there, in my kitchen. I know that sounds ludicrous, but let me assure you that I was not hallucinating, just sensing God's presence and his love for me in a very real way. I had never felt that before, nor have I felt it again. All that time the song was still playing in the background and I heard the lyrics, "My heart will _choose_ to say, Lord blessed be your

21

name." I realised there's a choice to be made and I'm going to make that choice today. I'm going to choose to trust him, I'm going to say yes to Jesus.

And I did.

The most striking change in me over the next few days was a hunger for the Bible. I'd always owned a Bible, but I'd never read it before. One day, battling anxiety, I opened it and came across Isaiah 41:10, such a well-known verse but I'd never read it before. My eyes drank it in: "So do not fear, for I am with you; do not be dismayed, for I am your God. I will strengthen you and help you; I will uphold you by my righteous right hand." I realised God was speaking to me clearly in a very personal way, the way that I would pick up the 'phone and chat to my mum. God was speaking through the Bible. And he could see and understand what no-one else could. He could see directly into my broken mind. Mental illness is isolating; it's difficult for a sufferer to describe their thought patterns so you feel cut-off, as if no-one understands. But as I read the Bible I saw that God understands. In fact, he's the only one who can truly understand because he created my inmost being and knew me before he formed me (Psalm 139). In one of the first revelations of his character, God describes himself as compassionate and gracious, slow to anger, abounding in love and faithfulness, *forgiving wickedness, rebellion and sin* (Exodus 34). How I needed God's forgiveness. Over and over, I read that God is full of compassion. The word "compassion" means to "suffer with." So God was with me and he was suffering with me. And so I began reading the Bible to hear God speaking compassion and comfort to me. I'd always been an early riser. Previously I would sit with a cup of tea and my thoughts, but now I sat with a cup of tea and God's word. In those early hours, when the house was quiet, I could be still and know God's peace as I immersed myself in the Bible.

Scripture revealed God in a new light. I learnt that God is not the angry, finger-wagging judge, I'd imagined but forgives us freely, remembering that we are dust (Psalm 103). I learnt that he's a father who watches and waits for all his wandering children to return, that he runs to welcome them, arms wide open (Luke 15). Best of all, I discovered the peace and power of prayer. I was able to talk to God, to pour out my heart to him because he listens, cares and understands. I saw from the Psalms that I could be completely honest and open with God, there was no need to pretend because nothing was hidden from him. He knew me better than I knew myself. The Psalms also taught me that I didn't need to talk to God in a formal polite tone. I could talk to God in plain English, the way I'd talk to a real person because he was real. So I placed a green plastic toddler chair which my kids had outgrown next to my desk. Every morning I imagined God was sitting in that chair - of course I knew he wasn't actually sitting there - but talking to him as if he was helped me to speak to him in a more natural way.

Another change was the healing of the skin infection. As a last resort the dermatologist had prescribed a steroid cream which worked. My skin healed completely. The dermatologist couldn't believe there was no scarring. God healed me of the skin infection, but for some reason, he didn't cure my mental illness completely, and that filled me with self-condemnation. 2 Timothy 1.7 says that God has not given us a spirit of fear, but of power, love, and a sound mind. I thought, how can I profess to be a Christian and still suffer from a mental illness? Why did I not have a sound mind? Was it a lack of faith? Was my illness sin? Was I possessed by an evil spirit? I had all these questions which I couldn't ask because I felt too ashamed and guilty.

But the Bible told me that Jesus won't break a bruised reed (Isaiah 42.3), that God sees us in all our frailties, all our wounds and weaknesses, and his heart for us is tender and compassionate. We're all bruised reeds in some way, some of us more than others. Our bodies and our minds are not perfect. This side of eternity there's heartache. We see this in the Gospels don't we? We see Jesus reaching out to people who are struggling to cope, people who are bruised reeds. If you're reading this and suffering from some form of mental or bodily affliction, if you're hurt or vulnerable, know that Jesus understands your pain, because he himself was despised and rejected, a man of sorrows, familiar with pain (Isaiah 53.3). I think Jesus was often very lonely. Even his closest disciples never really understood him, and when he needed them most they all abandoned him. Jesus suffered, that's why he can relate to us and share our suffering (Hebrews 4.15).

But more than walking with us through the hurts and disappointments, he has promised to redeem us. To bind up the brokenhearted, to provide beauty instead of ashes, joy instead of mourning, garments of praise instead of spirits of despair (Isaiah 61). Looking back on my life now, I can see that God has indeed redeemed those years. Sure, there are difficult times, but I'm not where I was: I no longer suffer crippling anxiety, I can organize my thoughts and I can write again.

The overarching promise of the Bible is redemption - joy will come in the morning because he is making all things new. And he is making all things new for me. He has given me a new heart, a heart to sing his praises and not be silent (Psalm 30). He has given me a new purpose for living, no longer for myself but for him. And he has given me a new task: the task of telling others the Good News about the wonderful grace of God (Acts 20.24).

The Bible tells me that I was created to know God, to live in a close personal relationship with him. You were created for that purpose too. My prayer is that you will say yes to Jesus today.

Ernie's story

A heart attack helped focus Ernie's thinking; that led him to experience Jesus, the like of which he has not had since and a peace that he had never had before.

At the time of writing I've been married to Ruby for over sixty years. I have eight children, numerous grandchildren and great-grandchildren. I've been involved in the church for over twenty years. In my working days I was a carpenter and worked on building sites.

When I was young my mother always used to take me to church, but as I grew up and got married and started a family I had no time for church whatsoever. However, when my brother came back from Australia I noticed a big change in him. He had always been what might be described as a "hard man." Eventually I found out that he had become a Christian. I was envious of him as he had a peace that I had never experienced. Indeed, despite being happily married and having a lovely family I knew something was missing so I started to read the Bible that he had sent me. I loved reading it.

One day my life took an unexpected turn. I was out in the street when I felt a very bad pain in my chest. However, as I walked on the pain left me. I got home and after telling my wife I thought no more about it. She however rang the doctor. After I had been examined and had tests done it was discovered that I had suffered a heart attack! This helped focus my thinking. I realised that even if I tried my best to live a very good life it was still not enough in the light of God's perfection and holiness. Only Jesus' death in my place could suffice. Eventually I prayed that Jesus would come into my life which he did. I knew my prayer had been answered as I had an incredible experience (of the like I have not had since) and now had a peace that I had never had before. In all the years since the Lord has always been there for me as he is faithful even when we are not. It is his grace that keeps me living for Him. I became a Christian at the age of sixty-two which proves it's never too late to make the most important change in life and accept Christ!

Helen's story

Raised in a Jewish family, famous singer Helen's New Age beliefs and interactions vanished overnight. A colleague, a book and much research led her to Jesus.

I was raised in a warm, musical, traditional Jewish family in the heart of a large Jewish community in Hackney, in the East End of London. Our extended family, although not a very orthodox group, was nevertheless totally Jewish in identity and heritage. My first recollections include wonderful annual festivals such as Passover, plus traditional rituals such as the lighting of candles on a Friday evening to welcome Shobbos (Shabbat).

I suppose I believed in God from my earliest days. I took His existence for granted. The state school I attended taught the Bible and I loved the Bible stories very much. However, because my school had a Jewish Headmaster and a large Jewish contingency among the pupils, we Jewish kids had separate RE (Religious Education) classes and assemblies. As a consequence I never heard of a New Testament or a Jesus until I was around six years of age. One day a non-Jewish girl came up to me in the playground in quite some distress and blurted out, "You killed Jesus Christ!" I was devastated and confused by this accusation. I had never killed anyone in my life, and who was this person with the strange name, Jesus Christ?

At fourteen, while still at school, I had my first hit record. That led me to go into show business, travelling the world, singing at many famous venues and having more hit songs, including "Walking Back to Happiness." I was carried along by all the fame, meeting celebrities and royalty and didn't give much thought to spiritual things until the late sixties. At that time, it seemed that everyone was searching for the "meaning of life." It was the "hippie" era. Thankfully I did not become involved with drugs or cults. However, members of my family had taken to visiting mediums, clairvoyants and other such folk to make contact (as they thought) with relatives who had died. Having always had a curiosity with life-after-death issues this fascinated me. I began to visit such people myself on occasions. I also started to read books and magazines about spiritism, Buddhism and all kinds of psychic phenomena. I developed a system of beliefs, over the years, which incorporated a little bit of this, a little bit of that - a smorgasbord of "isms" which, these days, would be called "New Age." To my own way of thinking I was not remotely involved in anything evil or sinister. I associated everything I believed in with God.

For quite a number of years I was comforted by what I had discovered. It seemed to fill a void in my life - until I turned forty years of age. A few months after this milestone birthday I woke up one morning and, to my own great surprise, I found I no longer believed in any of my "New Age" ideas. It's hard to explain but my belief in the supernatural had vanished overnight. Try as I might I could not believe in any of my "isms" any more. This presented a dilemma for me as I had always equated all my beliefs with God. Did this mean that there was no God? I found the whole thing very depressing. For the first time in my life I had nothing to believe in. My jazz and pop career was going well. I was in a relationship with the man who is now my husband. I was successful but inside I was empty. Looking back I can see that this was God's hand.

In those days my musical director was a man called Bob Cranham. He was a Christian and more than once he had spoken of what his "Lord" had done in his life. These were wonderful things but I couldn't consider them for myself because I am Jewish. This was the Gentile God blessing His people. In the midst of my turmoil I called in at his house one day to pick up some music. Now, neither Bob nor his wife knew anything of my inner struggle. Nobody did.

Bob dropped a bombshell that day. He said, "I'm thinking of giving up the music business." I asked him why. He said, "Because I believe God wants me to be a preacher." I thought to myself, "Oh dear. He thinks he's hearing from God." Here was a professional, sane and sensible top-quality musician, composer, song-writer, producer - and he's talking about giving up everything. Nothing I could say would sway him. He seemed so calm and sure and so willing to take this drastic step if, as he believed, God wanted it. I found myself becoming more and more impressed by how real and sincere his faith must be if he could surrender all that for his "Lord." I went home and told my boyfriend John how much I envied Bob. I had many opinions, but Bob had real convictions. I wanted what he had! I guess I was "provoked to jealousy."

I started to think about this Jesus constantly. I couldn't get Him out of my mind. Finally I lay awake one night and felt that I had nothing to lose. I whispered, "Jesus...?" I didn't know if I was going to be struck by lightning. "Are you really there? Are you really the Messiah? If you are, I want to know. Please show me." (I might as well mention that I had always believed that Jesus existed historically and that he was a Jew. I had never been able to equate the Jewish Jesus with the very un-Jewish artistic depictions of him -

blond hair, blue eyes, etc.) Nothing seemed to happen in my room that night but in the weeks that followed it seemed that everywhere I went I was bumping into things and people connected with this Jesus.

While all this was going on my band and I came back from doing a concert in Germany. When we arrived at the airport and were saying our farewells until the next gig Bob, my musical director, handed me a book. I was surprised to see that the cover was a picture of a Menorah (a seven-branched lampstand). The title of the book was, "Betrayed," written by Stan Telchin. The sub-title, in effect, said, "How would you feel as a successful fifty-year-old Jewish businessman if your daughter one day told you she believed in Jesus?!" "How did Bob know I was searching?!" I thought to myself. Of course he didn't know. Nobody knew.

The book was a total shock. I had heard about the odd Jewish person believing in Jesus but I had dismissed them all as weirdoes and cranks. Here was a book by a normal, successful Jewish businessman who believed in Jesus and I couldn't ignore it. Outwardly I showed no emotion. "OK, I'll read it," I said casually. My heart was thumping inside. I couldn't wait to read it. I found out later that Bob had wanted to give me the book for over a year, but the time had never seemed right - until now. How timely that book was.

It took me only a couple of hours to finish it. Stan Telchin was a pillar of the Jewish community in Washington D.C., successful in insurance, and a member of different Jewish organisations and committees. One day his daughter announced that she had accepted Jesus as her Messiah. After his initial shock and anger wore off he set out to prove her wrong. He spent months talking to Rabbis, pastors,

Jewish believers, Gentile believers, reading the Old and New Testaments, church history, Jewish history, you name it! After all that he ended up becoming a believer in Jesus as did every member of his family who went off to search for themselves.

I learned a great deal from reading this book. Most fascinating of all were the Messianic prophecies he listed. These are prophecies about the Messiah which are found in the Old Testament; the Tenach. I had never heard of them before. Now I learned that in the Law, the Prophets and the Writings there were dozens of specific predictions about a coming Messiah. I had known and loved the "hit" stories in the Old Testament about Abraham, Isaac, Jacob, Moses, David, Daniel etc. And I knew that we, the Jewish people, had been promised the Messiah but I never knew about these many, specific written prophecies.

For example, Stan spoke about Isaiah 9:6, where it's written, "For unto us a child is born, unto us a son is given..." I had always thought that verse was in the New Testament as I'd only ever seen it on Christmas cards. But there it was in Isaiah! One of ours! This verse goes on to say that this child would be called, "...Wonderful Counsellor, Mighty God, Everlasting Father, Prince of Peace." Mighty God! Is the prophet saying that the Messiah has to be God, somehow?

Then Stan quotes Isaiah 7:14, which states that the Messiah would be born of a virgin. I had always thought that talk of a virgin birth was most un-Jewish, but there it was in Isaiah, the Jewish prophet.

He also listed Micah 5:2, a verse from one of the so-called "minor prophets," which speaks of the Messiah being born in Bethlehem, even though he was also from eternity.

This was amazing enough until I read Psalm 22. It begins with the words "Eli, Eli, lama azavtani", which means, "My God, My God, why have you forsaken me?" I had seen enough films about Jesus to know that He cried these words out when He hung on the cross. What I didn't know was that the rest of the Psalm follows on to say "...they have pierced my hands and my feet. I can count all my bones... They have divided my garments among them and cast lots for my clothing." It seemed to be a picture of the crucifixion of Jesus. But how could it be? This Psalm was written a thousand years before Jesus and before crucifixion was even invented!

Finally I came face to face with Isaiah 53, the whole of which chapter speaks about one who is to come and take upon himself our sins and our punishment. "He was wounded for our transgressions, He was bruised for our iniquities, the chastisement for our peace was upon Him and with His stripes we are healed. All we, like sheep, have gone astray, each one of us has turned to his own way and the Lord has laid on Him the iniquity of us all." It seemed to be speaking about Jesus!

All of these prophecies appeared to be painting a picture that I wasn't sure I wanted to see. How come nobody ever showed me these things before? How come all I got was "You killed Jesus Christ!"?

I had to find out if these things were really in the Bible. I had to go and buy one. Where do you go to buy a Bible? WH

Smith, of course! I went into their "religious" section and was confronted with row upon row of Bibles! All shapes and sizes and types. Which one should I buy? There were so many to choose from. Why were there so many? After a long, careful search, I finally selected what seemed to be a straightforward choice - it was called "The Bible."

I took it home, opened up the Old Testament and there they were: prophecies about the Messiah! Dozens of them, speaking of Him coming both as suffering servant and victorious king. They all pointed, it seemed to me, to Jesus. Could it really be true? I had come this far - I couldn't go back now. I had to go on. With trepidation I opened, for the first time in my life, that forbidden book: The New Testament.

I didn't know what to expect. Would it be full of anti-Semitic poison? After all, look at what has been done against the Jews over the centuries in the name of Christ, by those claiming to be Christians. We figure they must get it from "their book."

Imagine my surprise when I opened up the New Testament and was greeted by the most Jewish thing I had seen outside of the Old Testament: the genealogy of Jesus. Not only was I unexpectedly greeted by a list of familiar names, but while reading Stan's book I had learned that the Messiah had to be descended from Abraham, Isaac and Jacob, had to be from the tribe of Judah and of the royal house of David. That was just for starters. All these names were there and many, many more, in this impeccable lineage of Jesus.

I discovered that the writers of the New Testament were Jewish too. I had always thought that James, Peter and John and co. were Englishmen. To my mind they couldn't be anything else with names like that! But I discovered that James was, in fact, Jacob, John was Yochanan, Mary was Miriam, Matthew was Mattityahu, Jesus is Yeshua which means "Salvation!" The New Testament is Jewish!

Greatly comforted, I began reading about these people, living in the Land of Israel, according to the Law of Moses. There was a temple and a priesthood - it was a continuation of the Old Testament. I didn't expect it to be like that. And then there was Jesus. He seemed to rise up out of the pages to me. I was drawn to Him: His words, His compassion, His miracles, His fulfilment of prophecy, His arrest and trial, His crucifixion and resurrection. I finished the Gospel of Matthew and had read halfway through the Gospel of Mark when the thought struck me that I was being too gullible and easily persuaded. It all seemed too perfect. This Bible, including the Old Testament, was, after all, translated by Christians. Maybe they had slanted it towards their way of thinking. I had to be sure. I had to get a "proper" Bible - a Jewish Bible.

I went to a little Jewish shop in Ilford that sold Judaica in the form of books, cards, religious clothing and so on. I was confronted yet again by wall-to-wall, floor-to-ceiling books. I stood there for what seemed an age, unable to find what I was looking for. The shopkeeper finally came over to me and asked, "May I help you?" "Yes," I replied. "I would like an Old Testament please." "How Old?" he asked. How embarrassed I felt! I realised my mistake: you don't go into a Jewish shop and ask for an Old Testament. There is no such thing as an Old Testament because there is no such thing as a New Testament. "You know what I mean!" I said. Of course he did. He reached up to a top shelf and brought down a book. "This is what you're looking for," he said.

It was a copy of the Tenach, The Holy Scriptures. I got it home and compared it with the Old Testament in my other Bible from WH Smith - and it was the same. I was so relieved. I was hoping it would be so.

I continued reading the New Testament. By the time I had read all four Gospels, I knew that Jesus was the fulfilment of all the Messianic prophecies. Jesus was and is the Messiah! This was the most wonderful realisation! But what do I do? This was controversial!

I telephoned Bob and said, "I think I'm on the verge of becoming a believer." He and his wife asked me over. I had so many questions. One of my main questions was to do with all my old smorgasbord of beliefs: where does God fit in with them? The answer is: He doesn't. Bob showed me from Deuteronomy right through to Revelation that all those things are an abomination to God and come under the heading of Occult. I learned that I had to repent of and renounce all of those practices.

I told Bob and his wife that I believed that Jesus was the Messiah, the Son of God and God the Son. I believed that He died on the cross, was buried and rose from the dead on the third day. I believed, but I still needed to understand - Why?

They showed me in the Bible, particularly in the letter to the Hebrews, how Jesus was the fulfilment of the sacrificial system, instituted by God when He brought the Israelites out of slavery in Egypt. Whenever God's Law was broken He graciously provided that atonement could be made by the shedding of the blood of an innocent substitute. We have all, Jews and Gentiles, broken God's Law and are under His condemnation and are deserving of His punishment. He still requires the shedding of blood. None of our good works or religious rituals can make us right with God.

Thankfully we don't have to slaughter animals for sacrifice anymore because all of those sacrifices were fulfilled in the once-for-all sacrifice of Jesus on the cross. He was the perfect Lamb of God. The moment He died on the cross, when He called out, "It is finished," the curtain in the Temple that divided the Holy Place from the Holy of Holies was torn in half, from top to bottom. Jesus has paid the penalty for sin and all those who repent and believe in Him can come into the presence of God as a cleansed and forgiven worshipper.

They explained that I needed to repent - to turn from my sin back to God. I learned that I was a sinner. We all are. Bob asked me if I would like to respond by praying and asking God to forgive me on the basis of what Jesus has done. Only He can forgive me and only the Blood of Jesus can atone for me. I could then commit my life to Him as my Lord and Saviour.

This I joyfully did on August 26th 1987 at 10:30 pm. Even though there were no thunderbolts or flashes of lightning I knew that my prayer was answered. I can't explain how I knew - I just did. It was all so real and true.

During my search I had begun to wonder: if I accepted the claims of Jesus and became His follower would I still be Jewish? On the way I had written to Stan Telchin along these lines. He assured me that I would be fulfilling my Jewishness by believing in Jesus, the Messiah of Israel and that I would be coming back to the God of Abraham, Isaac and Jacob.

What he said was true. The very reason that God created the Jewish nation was to point to the Messiah. This is the purpose of every Jew. I, along with many others, are fulfilling that very purpose by receiving Jesus as Messiah, Lord and Saviour.

Since repenting of my sins and receiving Yeshua - Jesus - I know that I have come out from under the condemnation of the Law: eternal separation from God and eternal punishment. We have all, Jew and Gentile, broken the Ten Commandments and are all guilty. Only by faith in the perfect sacrifice of Messiah Jesus can we be saved. I urge you to search the Scriptures and find out for yourself.

Howard's story

Howard's work as a cosmologist, his mother's deathbed smile and a father's revelation brought him back to Jesus.

I was dragged to church by my mother as a child but as soon as I was old enough to say, "No," I stopped going. My mother, who had a deep faith, never tried to cajole me to return; she never discussed her faith with me, she just lived it. She would go off to church each Sunday with my father and leave me in bed.

When I left home in my mid-twenties I used to return once a month for Sunday lunch. She never asked if I would come to church first. Sometimes I wished that she had so that occasionally I could say that I would, but as she didn't ask I didn't bother.

I got married, had children and led a very happy life with my family, working as a cosmologist, and no God although as I entered middle age I continued to wonder but still did nothing about it, and neither did my mother as far as I was aware. I was working on a paper on gravitational force. This force is determined by gravitational constant. Now if this constant varied by just one in ten to the power of sixty (that's one followed by sixty noughts) parts then we wouldn't exist. This is such a tiny amount. By way of comparison our bodies have fewer than one followed by fourteen noughts cells in them. Whilst I'm on the subject let's look at the expansion rate of the universe. A change in the cosmological constant of just one part in ten to the power of one hundred and twenty would cause the universe to expand more quickly or more slowly and again life would not be able to exist. Lastly, if the mass and energy of the universe, that's stuff like atoms and dark matter, were not evenly distributed to a precision of one part in ten to the power of ten to the power of one hundred and twenty-three it would be impossible to live in it. Our universe is so fine-tuned that, but for the fact that we do actually exist, life is statistically impossible.

The best explanation for why the universe is so fine-tuned for life is that it was designed that way.

Astronomer Fred Hoyle wrote, "A common sense interpretation of the facts suggests that a superintellect has monkeyed with physics...and that there are no blind forces worth speaking about in nature. The numbers one calculates from the facts seem to me so overwhelming as to put this conclusion almost beyond question."

Physicist Paul Davies wrote, "There is for me powerful evidence that there is something going on behind it all...it seems as though somebody has fine-tuned nature's numbers to make the universe. The impression of design is overwhelming." He has also argued that the faith that scientists have in the immutability of physical laws has origins in Christian theology, and that the claim that science is "free of faith" is "manifestly bogus."

My mother was always one of life's happy people; she was always smiling. But as she advanced through her eighties she became increasingly unable to look after herself and she became frustrated at not being able to carry out simple tasks. She stopped smiling. She eventually became totally dependent on my father and when he could no longer cope he found her a very pleasant nursing home near Tunbridge

Wells. By this time she was suffering from Parkinson's disease and had Alzheimer's amongst other medical issues.

My monthly visits became weekly ones. I would pick up my father every Saturday or Sunday afternoon and drive him to the nursing home to see my mother for an hour or so.

I had not seen her smile for over ten years. My father said that he hadn't either. Communication was difficult then impossible. We would just sit at the end of her bed and chatter to each other and occasionally throw out a comment or question to mother. She never responded. Most of the time her eyes were shut. She would open them occasionally when she was being fed.

One reads about people who claim to have died and then returned from the dead with stories of glimpses of the afterlife but I believe there's a difference between being properly dead i.e. biologically dead, and clinically dead where your heart has stopped but for a while you could still be resuscitated. No one who's died and seen God is going to be able to suddenly return to physical life and say, "It's true, I've seen him!" God is not going to reveal himself until someone is biologically dead. This makes what happened to my mother altogether more remarkable.

One Sunday we went early to the home as one of the nurses had 'phoned my father to say that mother was breathing very shallowly and that death was probably not far off. I had got up early that morning because something told me that I should but at the time I had no idea why. For the first time in years my father missed going to his Sunday morning service and instead I took him to see mother. We were let in and went straight to her room. She was in a bad way. She was lying in bed with her eyes shut. She looked dreadful. Her skin was a deathlike pallor. "Hello mother," I said as I perched on the side of the bed and took her hand. It was freezing cold and lifeless. There was no movement of any description, either in her eyes, her mouth, her fingers. Suddenly I got the shock of my life. She opened her eyes and was staring straight up. Then she sat bolt upright as if someone had put a pin in her back. With her eyes wide open staring at the wall beyond the end of the bed she did something that no one had seen for years. She began to smile. The most enormous, wide smile that took me back to when I was a child. That was how she had always looked at me before her illnesses got too bad. Then she fell back down against her pillow and by the time she had hit it her eyes were shut. But she was still smiling.

As father and I stood up wondering what to do one of the doctors came in. He quickly did a few checks and pronounced her dead.

I stood there in silence with the doctor and my father, my head spinning. Then I said, "I wonder what she was smiling at?" My father replied, "When you stopped going to church your mother started to pray for you even more. Every single day without once having a break. She hung on just long enough to show you that what God has prepared for those who love him is something to yearn for and as she died she saw it and wanted you to know."

The following week I went back to church and have been going ever since. When I die I want to see what mother saw.

Jim's story

Former professional motorcycle racer Jim became a Christian and within one year witnessed God's healing at work in another person's life though prayer.

I spent about ten years of my life as a motorcycle racer, starting when I was eighteen years old. The latter five years I was sponsored by many companies as I was quite successful. In 1964 I was rated the third top rider in the country in all three classes that I raced in - 250, 350 and 500cc.

I knew Bernie Ecclestone quite well. I used to work with him and rode his motorbikes. He wanted to get in on the bike racing scene. He brought a couple of Nortons into my workshop for me to work on. He asked me to ride them for him but I gave them back telling him that they weren't fast enough. Mine were faster than his! However I did ride other of his bikes for him quite a bit. He was a really nice bloke. On one occasion I took one of his bikes and won. When I returned his bike I gave him the winnings. "It's quite a bit of money," I told him. "It's your bike." However he said to me, "You rode it, you won it. I've got the advertising. You keep the winnings."

Bernie used to race 500cc Coopers but stopped after several accidents. His long career path started in Bexleyheath. He worked for a Mr Fred Compton who used to have a motorcycle shop. Bernie used to clean the bikes. One day Bernie said to Fred, "If I had my own bikes could I put them in your showroom and sell them?" Fred said, "Yes, that will be alright." However Bernie did such a good job cleaning and speccing his own bikes, better than those he was selling for Fred, that they changed the name of the business to "Compton and Ecclestone." He was a very good salesman and I always found him a very nice guy.

At one important race, the British Championships, at Oulton Park, I had a nasty crash. The motorcycle caught alight and I was carted off to hospital unconscious. Afterwards I didn't remember much about what had happened. I had banged my head but wasn't too badly injured. However the doctors wouldn't discharge me until they knew that I was okay. In those days there was quite a simple test. If you could walk straight down a white line then you were good enough to drive and you were told that you could go home. I spent about a week in hospital before I could walk in a straight line and off home I went.

The next big race to come up was the Manx Grand Prix. I was tipped to win that as one of the favourites along with a few friends of mine. Motorcycle racing is a bit like a circus travelling around the country. You meet the same people at every track and you get to know them. Consequently you become very good friends with some of them. A few of us got together. Because of the damage round my collarbone and broken wrist from my crash at Oulton Park I couldn't go to the Isle of Man and compete. Some of my friends who were also top riders and tipped to win came to see me before they went off to race. It was pouring with rain in the Isle of Man. One of them, Fred Neville, led the 350cc race all the way until the last lap when he fell off at Greeba Castle. He lost control on the wet road and crashed into a stone wall. He sadly died on the way to hospital. He was twenty-six years old. I was then listening to the 500cc race that another friend, Roy Mayhew, was in. He was in about fourth place, doing well, keeping up with the front runners when on the last lap he disappeared. I didn't know where he had gone and there wasn't much on the radio apart from he had probably broken down somewhere on the mountain, which he had. He then decided to come back and race at Brands Hatch. One of the things to do, after a big event, was if you could quickly get to a local track, as all the top guys were still on their way home, you could earn a bit of money. This was something that Roy used to do. He turned up at Brands Hatch but crashed at the end of the main straight approaching Paddock Bend. His back wheel suddenly lifted. He went off the circuit and the bike threw him off before landing on top of him. He was rushed to hospital but died that night.

After these two fatalities of close friends of mine I sat back and wondered, "What on earth is going on? What's it all about?" People were getting killed left, right and centre and I was still alive. I began to think about retiring. I didn't really want to and felt that I shouldn't just because I had had a crash. I then received a letter. It was from BMW. In it I was being asked whether I would ride their works' BMW in a 24-hour endurance race at Barcelona. It was in the streets at Montjuïc, a beautiful but challenging race on one of the most dangerous street circuits in the world. I replied that I would so off I went. I came third but was then disqualified because the bloke who was helping, the other team rider, fell off on the last lap. He got up and finished but was told that because he hadn't completed the lap in a competitive time, even though we had a big lead, we were disqualified. After that I decided to pack up racing motorcycles and move over to cars.

I went out and did everything that many other young people do. Money wasn't a problem because I had been quite well paid for my racing. I bought myself a Jaguar and decided that I needed to find myself a girlfriend. However nothing seemed right, nothing was working out; I didn't know what to do.

It was at that point that I started to go out with a girl that attended Christ Church, Chislehurst in Lubbock Road. After a while she suggested that I go along and play a bit of table-tennis with the young lads, so I did. I didn't think they were much good at it but this was probably due to a huge competitive streak within me. On one occasion one of the leaders suggested to me that I might like to come and help. It was then that my involvement became more regular with weekly visits to this youth group called "Pathfinders." I would help with whatever they needed help with. It was there that I met a leader called Stuart Lock and we became friends.

At one point it became quite interesting because a load of motorcyclists found out where I lived and what I was doing and so decided they should come and say, "Hello." Lubbock Road became something of a race track. The neighbours were beginning to get a bit agitated so I had to get all the bikers together and have a word.

I started to become more and more involved with Pathfinders and began to take them out. We took them to watch car racing at Wimbledon Stadium. The previous year I was racing a car there for someone. I raced in an international race with competitors from the Netherlands and I happened to win it. It was called "The Golden Hands Trophy." I beat them all even though I had a Ford and they all had Porsches and suchlike. That year I was in the same race and I thought that they would all want to get their own back. I felt that I wouldn't have a chance. I organised a coach to take the Pathfinders to Wimbledon to watch the race. I made it through the heats and found myself in the final. I won it! I was presented with a nice trophy by a famous singer. I can't remember his name. He ripped his trousers once at the height of his fame, that's all I can remember about him.

Although car racing was safer than bikes, eventually I decided to stop racing cars as well. I then had more time to concentrate on what I was doing with the church. In February 1964, with the help from Stuart, I gave my life to the Lord. I was then invited to speak at Central Hall, Westminster alongside Cliff Richard and Billy Graham. The place was packed! I was quite frightened when I walked out and saw how many people were there. I gave my testimony about what led me to become a Christian.

I still had my workshop in Chislehurst, GB Speed Equipment, where I worked on engines including my own. I would build racing engines both for cars and bikes, grinding cylinder heads to get more power and stuff like that. I would modify parts for customers so that they could get that little bit extra speed. I would do work for tuning shops, producing wide wheels, replacing cam shafts, all in my little workshop in Royal Parade. One day I got a chunk of metal in my eye and had to go to hospital to get it sorted out. I went to Queen Mary's Hospital, Sidcup. Whilst I was sitting in the waiting room I noticed a girl with a cut. It was the longest cut I had ever seen, right up one of her arms. I sat there wondering how on earth she could have received such a large injury when she was taken off to be treated as was I. However, we re-emerged both at the same time. I said, "Hello, I'm Jim. I was looking at you earlier and saw that you had a really nasty cut. Would you mind telling me how it happened?" She replied, "No I don't mind you asking. I did it myself. I just get depressed. I feel lost and don't know what to do so I damage myself." I said to her, "Don't you think the Lord could help you?" She told me that her name was Beth, her father was a churchwarden in a local church and the church had prayed for her already. I told her, "You can't have too much prayer, you know that don't you?" She then suggested that I could pop round to her house anytime where I could meet her mum and dad and have a chat. She told me where she lived. Back home I told Stuart and he said that he would come with me whenever I decided to go.

Stuart and I were out one day having a drink in a pub near Brands Hatch. It was The Plough in Eynsford on the River Darent. I mentioned Beth and said that she lived around there somewhere but I couldn't remember where exactly. When we were back in the car and driving away I saw the name of the house. "That's it!" I said. "So let's pop in," said Stuart. "You told me that she said to come round anytime." We drove in through a large pair of gates and up the drive. Suddenly we saw in front of us a massive house with tennis courts and loads of people milling about. I said to Stuart, "Just turn round and get out of here!" However Beth saw us. She ran across the grass and grabbed us. "I'm so pleased to see you!" she exclaimed. We got out of the car whereupon she said that we should go and meet her dad and speak to him. I told him who we were and asked him if he had any problem with us praying for and over his daughter. He said that that was fine so we got a small group together to pray for her.

We kept in touch with her but her illness just got worse. She was self-harming more and more so she had to go back to hospital and then she was placed in a psychiatric hospital. However our group decided that we wouldn't give up on her so continued to have weekly meetings where we would pray for her.

One Saturday afternoon at about four o'clock we were praying away when one of the girls started to mumble. Tongues suddenly broke out amongst the group. Everybody stopped and looked. We were a bit bewildered. I looked at Stuart, "I think it could be a sign. We're going to get in the car and we're going to drive to the mental health hospital where she is and we're going to pray for her there." We piled into Stuart's car as best we could and went off to the hospital. At the reception we said that we had come to see Beth. She came running towards us with her arms open wide. We said, "Beth! Beth! Beth!" Before we could say anything further she said, "I have some wonderful news! This afternoon, about four o'clock, suddenly I felt something happen to me! I'm free! I'm not going to hurt myself anymore. I want to go home! I'm changed!"

We prayed with her again and then eventually off she went home. This was much harder than it sounds because in those days once it had been decided that the psychiatric hospital was where you should be then that's where you stayed and you didn't get out. However Beth was properly cured; she left the hospital and went back to her life. This all happened within one year of my becoming a Christian. Things just seemed to happen.

She was a team sport player for Kent and the last I heard she was keeping well.

John's story

Jesus' conversation from the cross reduced sawmill worker John to floods of tears twice - then a prayer that he prayed resulted in a sensation that left him in no doubt that he had just met with God.

I was born and raised in the area known as The Meadows, Nottingham, into a working class background with one brother, Michael, just a year younger. When I was around sixteen years old, in my last year at school, I began to wonder what life was all about.

Is there such a thing as God?

We had not attended church or Sunday school as children and therefore had no concrete religious views. Indeed, my brother and I knew very little of what the Bible said at all. My dad, who was a schizophrenic, had attended a Catholic school, a fact that he only ever mentioned in a disparaging fashion. He believed that God was an astronaut having read such things written by Swiss author, Erich von Däniken. My mother, a manic depressive, believed that there was a God and believed in Jesus Christ. As a girl she had gone to Sunday school. She spoke with great affection of the day she was dressed all in white for her confirmation; it was one of the highlights of her life. Unfortunately her beliefs and understandings were very muddled. She had never gone to church during my brother and my lifetimes.

The Big Bang theory was in its heyday. Taught at school all my mates believed that this life was your lot and the only almighty was the full stop that came with death. I, however, struggled to believe in a purely evolutionary theory. The world is too amazing and beautiful to be due to a freak of nature. Yet I could not be sure; I just did not know. I had a number of discussions with my mates about God, whether there was a spiritual realm and what happens to you when you die. After one such occasion I remember going to bed proper confused, my mind in turmoil wondering about the things we'd spoken of. I lay there thinking, "What if I die in my sleep tonight?" It was a cold thought, but I supposed that if you just die, then you would not think or feel anything, would you? That night, probably for the first time, I prayed on my own and not repeating something in a school assembly. It was a very simple prayer but from the heart. "Oh, God," I said, "if you are there, let me know you." I woke up in the morning, went to school and just continued with my day to day life.

There was no expectation of young people in this area but there was plenty of employment at that time. I left school and went to work in a saw mill at a local woodyard. It was there where I met a guy about the same age as me. His name was Pete Crosby. I was seventeen at the time. It got around that he read the Bible. I made a bee-line for him and asked him if it were true, did he read the Bible? "Yes," he replied. The strange thing was, instead of asking this guy questions such as, How can you know God exists? Where is He? and so on I just called out God to him for all the injustices of the world and life in general etc. Then after a few days I began to question myself. Why was I doing this? Did I really want to know if there was a God? It was certainly refreshing to hear someone who seemed absolutely certain there was but I was not giving him a chance to put his case forward. Though I had no answers for my behaviour I resolved to give the guy a chance in the future. He was okay, born in Mansfield, followed that team, hey, you've got to admire that. I got to know him a bit and we became quite good work mates.

Pete encouraged me to read the Bible. I had to borrow one of his, a New Testament. This was another first. It was the first time I had ever read the Bible! I kept it shoved down the side of the settee. This would mean that no one in my family would see me reading it because otherwise they would take the mick out of me. When I was on my own I would fish it out. Everything went down there: Pencils, crayons, bike wheel, ahh Bible.

I became quite engrossed with the Gospels. Jesus seemed an alright guy; he tried to help people and get along with them even whilst being unafraid to speak his mind. I distinctly remember reading the bit about Jesus on the cross and the two thieves at his side. One of them starts taking it out of Jesus, joining in with the mockers who were scoffing that he was unable to save himself let alone anyone else. The other one tells him to shut up because they are there for the wrong they have done. Then the other one turns to Jesus and asks if he would remember him when he gets into his kingdom, Jesus replies, "Truly I tell you, today you will be with me in paradise." All at once floods of tears came running down my face. I felt enraged. I was angry because I had got all emotional over a stupid story. I threw the book into an empty chair. My difficulty was that Jesus could forgive someone while he himself was in agony, and that he would be dead in an hour or so. The other criminal was not going to be able to do anything with Jesus' message, what was the point in forgiving him, what good works was he going to do? It seemed senseless and perhaps a little unfair. Needless to say I told no one of this.

Intrigued by what had happened to me, and to prove to myself that this was some silly emotional outburst, a couple of days later I went to reread the same passage. I really could not believe it; the same thing happened again! This time I prayed, in earnest, obviously turning into a religious maniac, the second time in the matter of a few years. I said, "If Jesus' death is anything to do with me, I am sorry." I finished reading the Bible and had become pretty well convinced that there was a God and this made me feel content. My work mate Peter moved to The Jesus Centre in Birmingham and said that he would keep in touch by letter.

One Easter I saw an advert in the Daily Mirror. It was offering a free Bible if you wrote off to some guy named Billy Graham. This I did and within a few days it arrived. I looked at the back of it to see if there were any maps or suchlike. Actually what there was was a load of stuff on what the death of Jesus meant as well as sin and so on. Quoted on one of the back pages was the well-known verse, Revelation 3:20, "Behold, I stand at the door and knock. If anyone hears my voice and opens the door, I will come in to him and eat with him, and he with me." A note said that Jesus was standing at the door of my life wanting to come in and share his life with mine. There was also a prayer set out that I could use to ask Jesus to come into my life. The prayer consisted of confessing that I was a sinner, thanking Jesus for dying for my sin, asking him to come into my life and giving thanks to him for the gift of the baptism of the Holy Spirit. I remembered the first prayer I had prayed a couple of years ago. "Oh God, if you are there let me know you." I was now getting used to praying so I went up to my bedroom and knelt on the floor, because that's what you're supposed to do I thought. I pressed the pages of the Bible open so it didn't keep flopping shut and I recited the words of the prayer.

As I stood back up the sensation that I felt left me in no doubt that I had just met with God. I felt so elated that God would come into my life. Me. A nobody, just some ordinary guy that lives down the street.

I was now nineteen years old then but it was still nearly a year before I crossed the threshold of a church. I had continued writing to Pete and I had been telling him of how I was terrified at the thought of going to church. I felt that I would be the odd one out as all those who went to church had been brought up to do so. All the people there would be really nice and good and I would stick out like a sore thumb. I continued to read the Bible fervently.

One evening a knock came on the door. A man stood in the doorway with shoulder-length hair and a beard. I thought, he's come in person! But it wasn't Jesus, it was a Frenchman named Jean-Claude. He was a friend of Pete's. He asked if I would like to go to the church youth club with him that night. Ironically, all these years later I find that I spend most of my life in that church trying to persuade others to do the same. I sometimes wonder if this is God's sense of humour?

Anyway, I went to the youth club and the following Sunday morning I attended a church service for the first time in my life. I felt an overwhelming sense of the presence of God. I adored the hymns. They were so articulate and full of passion I began to use them for my own personal prayers. My favourite was Wesley's "O Thou Who Camest from Above." The verse I used to pray was,

"...kindle a flame of sacred love
upon the mean altar of my heart.

There let it for thy glory burn
with inextinguishable blaze..."

I too had my reasons and excuses for not becoming a disciple but this is how I came to be a follower of Jesus. I now want other ordinary people like me to come to know God in their life too. I want ordinary people like you to experience the life-changing power of the Holy Spirit and become a follower of Jesus.

Kevin's story

From a horrific cult via body-building, steroids, ecstasy (counterfeit Holy Spirit) and more drugs to jail where eternity dropped on him. Kevin was transformed and now leads others through the power of the Holy Spirit.

I was born into a horrific cult where I was separated from the world as a family. I couldn't mix with anyone. The cult believed that if you were not with them then you're outside their world and so you're all destined to hell. The fear of that was what trapped you in this cult. If you did anything that they thought, or the Universal Leader thought, was bad they would kick you out. However they would not only kick you out from the church but they would also remove you from your family, your friends, your life - everything that you had lived by. This is what happened to my dad so I could no longer see him and he couldn't see me; he was told not to come near our family because if he did do it he would make us unclean and we would have to go to hell with him. Therefore I grew up in this oppressive environment. It messed me up. In the end my mum said that we had to get the family back together again. I had a brother and a sister and they needed my dad and I needed my dad so we all left the cult. The leaders came to my mum and dad and told them, "We've got to take your brother;" my brother was fourteen years old, "we can't allow him to stay with you because if he stays with you then you're taking him to hell." They gave him up because they were brainwashed into doing that.

Just to give you an idea of how bad it was: when my mum's mum died the cult leaders wouldn't let my mum go to the funeral, furthermore they wouldn't tell my dad that his mum had died until four months after her death. If any of the family or cousins or anybody that was in the cult ever saw us in the street they would rebuke us or they would cross over the road. We were convinced that we were now on our way to only one place - and that place was hell. We had no family and no friends; I was eleven at the time. I've grown up in this and all of a sudden I was let out in the big wide world. I had been locked in a place where I didn't have a TV, I didn't have friends and I didn't understand anything about the world so now I was like a kid in the sweet shop but I was still messed up so I couldn't relate. Over time I got so fed up with my life that I said that I needed to change something. I believed in my small mind that if I went to the gym I could build my muscles up and look a bit tougher; I would get some friends and change the way I looked. I would get a girlfriend - just normal things that a sixteen or seventeen-year-old lad would want. I had just had enough.

I met this guy and he was massive! I asked him, "How do I get to be the size that you're at?" Straightaway he said to me, "Steroids."

Now you've got to remember that I had no filters because I didn't really know the world. It was like me asking, "Where did you get that pint of milk from, which shop did you get it from?" because I wanted some. When he told me where I could get steroids from within days I was taking these pills and within a week I was injecting myself. Then I started partying with these guys, going out to clubs and I began to take drugs - this was the rave scene in the '90s. When I took my first tablet of ecstasy it was amazing. It's meant to be - this is counterfeit Holy Spirit; it's sent by the Devil to make me feel good about myself. However, when I got into taking drugs all of a sudden when I came back down to where I was before I took them I went way deeper and it exposed the hurt locker in my life. All of a sudden I had pain that needed soothing so it wasn't just about the weekend - I needed to do it during the week. No sooner had I started smoking weed than I was doing speed, I was doing LSD, I was taking everything I could possibly have. I had been teetotal for eighteen years but in two short years my life went from that to complete, total destruction - but I was having the time my life. I finally had all my heart's desires which was friends and also respect. I was big! All of a sudden those kids that used to take the mickey out of me in school started respecting and fearing me.

I was going to all sorts of parties. One night I was in a club where we knew the doorman. He attacked the drug dealer in the club and took all his drugs off him then gave them to us. We sold them and from that day on we made it into a business and within the space of about three months we were moving all the drugs for the biggest nightclub in Liverpool, in fact in England and one of the biggest in Europe. Now I had money. It was amazing! I looked good, I had friends, I was off my head all the time and it was everything my heart desired.

Then it all changed because the police caught up with me. I was sent to jail.

You need to understand what I had come out of. I was a messed-up kid that had never had the chance to adjust to life and when I did have the chance I filled it with drugs and escapism. Even in school I couldn't be educated; I was autistic and the school didn't want me anymore. When you're twenty-one years old and you're sent to a jail and you've never really been in trouble with the police before, you've never come from a life like that, all I can say is it's not the prison, it's not the four walls that you're locked in - it's your mind and that's the worst prison of all. With prison you know when you're going in and you know when you're getting out but when you're locked in your mind, the four walls of your mind, it could be forever and when you're banged up twenty-three hours a day you've just your mind. The best way to describe it to people who've never been in jail is that you know when you've got a bill or a concern or had an argument that you've got worries about, you go to bed tired and you start thinking about whatever it is and it mushrooms to the point that you can't easily sleep and then you wake up the next day and get back to life? Well, in jail you're locked up for twenty-three hours a day with just the thought of dread and pain and fear and, "I'm not going to survive this and my mum and dad will die and I won't get to see them in the way that they didn't get to see their mum and dad." What I didn't realise at the time was that the Devil knew that one day I would be writing this for this book and that he'd been sent to kill, steal and destroy my life. I didn't know that then and I got in so deep that I was getting close, if not there already, to despair; I was a broken person.

I thought I'd had a bit of a reprieve when I got a job in the servery. This included collecting the trays. This meant that I was the only person out of their cell. It meant I could pass drugs from one cell to another. Within moments I got a call, "Take this from forty-six to forty-one." I was now dealing drugs again but this time in jail. However the only benefit I was getting for moving them, it was heroin, was that I wouldn't get cut up or stabbed. I'm in this jail messed up already and now I'm moving drugs. I'm trapped by the fact that if I don't move them someone's going to hurt me.

One night this voice from behind me says, "Stop right there." It was a prison officer. He had caught me whilst I was putting something into a door. He looked at me and said, "You've got two choices: you can get in front of me and walk down the stairs or I'm ringing this bell and you can be carried down by four men. He took me into a room and said, "We know you're moving smack around this prison. We know and we're watching you and when we catch you you're going to get another five years added to your sentence." I was an utter mess anyway and now I had a choice: I either accept that I'm going to get caught and have an extra five years added to my sentence or I'm going to stop but get hurt.

I was broken; I was at the end of my rope. My mum arranged to send this guy in to see me. I just wanted to get out of the oppressive nature of the environment that I was in. This guy started talking to me about Jesus. I didn't want to know about Jesus, after all Jesus was the guy who messed my family up. I blamed God for the fact that I was in that jail because it was all part of the same thing. However I wasn't able to speak because I was so broken so I just listened as he told me about a Jesus who loved me, about a Jesus who would meet me where I was. I now reckoned I had two choices left: one was to kill myself and the second one this guy was about to tell me. He said, "When you get to the end of your rope just say this..." He said, "Jesus save me." What he didn't realize was that I was already there with the rope. When I got back to my cell I waited for the lights to go down then I waited for my cellmate to fall asleep below me. Under my covers I just said, "Jesus, if you're real save me."

Nothing happened. Typical. Nothing happened but what you have to remember is we've got a specific God because he wanted me back in the very same place where the worst thing that ever happened to me was which was landing three outside the door where I had been caught. That was terrifying. I quickly fell asleep, usually I wouldn't fall asleep so fast. The next morning when I woke up I realised that I had been asleep deeper than I had ever been before; I was late for my job so I got up and got started on my work soon forgetting about what had been going on during the night. However, in no time at all I was back on the landing and the dread started pouring onto me because I knew the prison officers were watching me.

I was just petrified but, as I said, our God is a specific God and I was about to realise why He didn't come and meet me at the moment I said my prayer in the cell, effectively alone in that dark room. He wanted me back in the very same place which was when I was at my lowermost. He wanted to take the ground back in my honour. When I got back to that place where I got caught by that prison officer, delivering whatever it was through the door, this presence just fell on me. Heaven opened up inside of me; eternity just dropped on me. It was like the roof had been blown open by the sun and the sun was shining through but only hitting me. All the hairs on my arm looked like I had got angels standing in the presence of God and I had goose bumps on my skin like bubble wrap. All the pain and all the suffering just left me. There was no guessing; I knew right there and then that this person that was making himself known to me was Jesus. He just poured all this love and all this peace and all this presence and every fiery dart of the Devil just disappeared in a moment. I had been in the worst place I had ever been, feeling the worst I ever had, but now feeling better than I had ever known. I had not a drug in my system that could make me higher than I then felt. I knew it wasn't a drug and I knew who it was. It was Jesus. I was saved. I was set free. When I came out of jail, first and foremost what's important to remember is that when my mum saw me again she thought I had lost my mind because I was high as a kite on Jesus. She had never stopped praying for me. I was transformed in a moment, a completely different person, almost delirious because I couldn't shut up about what Jesus had done, the person I had met and how powerful and strong I was.

The incredible thing is within a week I was transferred out of that jail so I never got the chance to be asked to take anything to anywhere again.

If I had gone sooner I would have gone to a jail that would have been softer and so I may never have got to rock bottom and called out for Jesus.

When I got out of jail my probation officer said to me, "You've got to do something." She convinced me to go to college because there wasn't a job that I could do. I was autistic and couldn't be educated but in four years I was on a degree course and I was the highest achieving student. Within six years I had become a chartered surveyor. I had gone from At Her Majesty's Pleasure to the Royal Institute of Chartered Surveyors. Now God's in the game of transformation and he wasn't finished there.

Two years into my job I got a call. It was Merseyside Police. Now the last time I spoke to them I was being interviewed so my heart's racing because nobody knows I've got a past and I'd been in all sorts of trouble. I take the call wondering if it might be one of the lads just having a joke. "Is that Kevin Cockburn?" "Yes." "This is Merseyside Police," and it was. I'm now wondering why on earth they are calling me. The caller said, "You advise on properties don't you?" I said, "Yes," so they told me that they wanted to sell Main Bridewell which is a prison in Liverpool. They asked if I would advise on the site and put it on the market. What they didn't realise was that Main Bridewell was the very same prison I had spent time in. Incredibly I had been retained by the police as a criminal, now I was being retained by the police as a professional. I remember taking the keys and God saying to me, "These are the keys that locked you up and now I'm putting them back in your hand because I'm going to use you to go back into jails to set people free in the way that I've set you free."

I'm in jail meeting these prisoners. I go up to them and say, "You know I've been where you are. I've been messed up and Jesus came and saved me." Sometimes they would say, "That's nice." Others would laugh or tell me, "I'm not interested." This is fine because I plant a seed and somebody else will water it and God will win the growth but God gave me a revelation and the revelation was around faith and risk. What that actually means, I heard it in a conference, is that somebody asked me, "How do you spell 'faith'?" He said that the answer was R-I-S-K. I didn't really know what that meant but God started showing me over time what that looked like. He took me to the story about when Peter walks on water. Only two people walk on water in the Bible and one of them was Peter. He was the only one out of the twelve that took a risk and he was the only one out of the twelve that experienced the miracle while the other eleven watched what he was experiencing. Jesus at no point said, "Peter, get out of the boat and get over here."

Peter said, "Can I come to you?" I reckon he said it not wanting to go to Jesus. There was a storm and it's kicking off all over. I imagine when Jesus says, "Yeah, come to me," Peter then realises that Jesus was not making his way over to the boat to help him and his heart began to pound but it's too late now and Jesus has said, "Come." You can imagine him calling and Peter getting out the boat. The waves are going everywhere and Peter's just looking at Jesus asking, "You're sure, you're sure?" Then Peter puts his foot down and all of a sudden the water solidifies and he's walking on water.

A lot of people will use that story to think about where your focus is; look at Jesus and you won't be defined by the waves and you walk on water but I saw it as if you take a risk you're going to experience a miracle. Signs and wonders follow those who believe. Don't you want to experience a miracle? Be ready to take a risk, be ready to get out of your boat.

Back visiting prisoners in jail and I want the scariest, ugliest-looking, horriblest criminal I can see who hates God. God didn't let me down. This fellow comes out. He's bigger than me, twice the size of me, like a bulldog chewing a wasp. He didn't want to speak to anybody let alone me let alone hear about Jesus. I went straight over to him with my heart going. I told him that I had been in jail. I told him I have struggled like he is. As soon as I mentioned Jesus he looked at me and said, "No." However, I'm there and I'm about to take a risk. Usually I would then stop as it's all about planting the seed, telling people about Jesus and letting God do what he needs to but sometimes we can use that as a cop-out to not take the risk and not get out of the boat. I decided that it was my turn to step out, put my foot down and give God a platform; I didn't know what I was about to say. No sooner had I opened my mouth than scripture started coming out. "You know Jesus loves you, do you know he thought you were worth dying for, you know he knew you before the foundation of the earth, you know he's pursued you all your life, you know he wants to relate and all of a sudden this guy starts going, "What's going on?" His whole countenance had changed; he's being touched by the Holy Spirit; he's being released by the power of the Gospel that I'm sharing over this life in a dark prison. This guy didn't want to know about Jesus. I said to him, "Can I put my hand on you?" He said, "Yes." I said to myself, "More God." You can see it in him. He says, "What's going on? This is amazing!" The guy gives his life to Jesus.

Now I'm on a roll; I want to increase the risk. I saw a Muslim that I had been talking to. I went over to him because I've had a session with him earlier on and we were talking about Zacchaeus. This is when Jesus comes and Zacchaeus takes him to his house and Jesus says, "Salvation has come to this house." I ask the Muslim, "Why did Jesus say, 'Salvation has come to this house'?" The Muslim turned around and just blurted out, "Because Jesus is the Son of God."

It says in the Book of Joel and in the Book of Acts that in the last days, "...the spirit will fall out on ALL flesh..." Nobody special but everyone special. So I'm looking at this Muslim and I have these people behind me. I say to him, "Why did you say that because you don't believe Jesus is the Son of God, you believe he's a prophet?" I didn't give him a chance to answer. I said, "Flesh and blood didn't reveal that to you." No sooner had I started speaking over him than he's sliding down his chair. He then gives his life to Jesus.

Now the upshot of that story is seven people got saved because I got out my boat and took a risk. When you look at the life that I've led, all that I've been through and the pain and the trials and the tribulations it was to get me ready to become so heavily minded that I'm super natural and earthly amazing because of who it is that lives in me. God is amazing. God's in the game of transformation and if he can do that to me and my life he can do it to anybody.

Laura's story

Laura spoke with spirits and became a spiritualist but things didn't go well, then they went from bad to worse; she prayed to Jesus and the spirits disappeared, following that she received deliverance and her life changed as a result, rescuing her from a deep, dark pit. Jesus has truly done a work of transformation in her life.

Spirituality in your Family
You have probably heard of alternative therapies such as receiving Reiki massage, healing energies, balancing chakras, using crystals, witchcraft spell books, tarot cards, psychic development classes as well as things like automatic writing or ghost hunts. You, or someone you know, will no doubt be invited to try some of these. There are many such spiritually-empowered practices, so common and popular in every realm of society now even though, just a few decades ago, most people were wary of them.

Very few, even well-known psychic mediums, would dare use Ouija boards for example. Nowadays all of these are far more available and accepted. But, as scholars, doctors and countless other people including former occultists, can confirm, opening supernatural doors can have serious and disastrous results. Worse still, such activity affects our soul forever, whether or not we feel it.

"He reached down from on high and took hold of me; He drew me out of deep waters. He rescued me from my powerful enemy, from my foes, who were too strong for me." Psalm 18:16-17.

If you saw a child drowning, you would want to rescue them. If someone close to you began to experience unwanted dangerous paranormal activity, would you know how to advise them? Could you help set them free? It's so important to know. This is occurring more often in our world. But few talk about it for fear of what others will think, being labelled delusional or mentally ill. Like sexual assault or domestic abuse, many who suffer keep silent about it.

Sucked into the paranormal
This is my personal story. Although it may seem unusual and dramatic, it's not unique at all. Tragically it's becoming more common, frequent and widespread.

The supernatural fascinated me since childhood. Being a psychic medium my mother was involved in New Age mysticism and seeking spirits and spirit guides through spiritualism. The focus on ghost stories in children's books and TV programmes fed my interest. My aunt and I saw a UFO when I was a child, adding to the intrigue I felt.

From then, and all through my teens and young adult life, even although I believed "good aliens" would visit and unite the world in peace, I had nightmares involving what is commonly termed "night terrors" or "sleep paralysis." I would dream of aliens attempting to abduct me and of a global invasion from alien crafts, succeeding in killing the entire human race.

One day, while my mum was out walking our dogs, a medium approached her saying he could sense her clairvoyant capabilities that she should develop further. He invited her to séances at a spiritualist church in Glasgow,

Scotland where we lived. She was delighted that he saw her potential. After visiting several times she was intrigued and soon joined that church. I went along and soon joined too. The mediums would drift into trances, then apparently channel dead people directly with visual materialisation and audible manifestation of voices or, most often, by telepathic communication.

These spirits genuinely seemed to be spirit guides and the ghosts of dead relatives, giving accurate personal messages to the audience. The vast majority of mediums are sincere, not charlatans using trickery or guesswork. Spirit entities can be extremely accurate and do indeed know a lot of information. They can also predict the future and produce real miracles of healing and so on.

What spirits and guides taught us
We also knew that alleged dead people and aliens often appeared together or would claim to be contacting us from UFOs, explaining they all knew each other and existed together in the same spiritual realms.

Spirit guides spoke to mediums, or those called Light Workers. They claimed to be ancient alien gods, interdimensional beings, from distant star systems that had created humankind. They said there were thousands of different alien races, good and bad, either helping or hindering mankind, from their myriad of astral planes. Today mediums report they are contacted by even more alien races.

They have names for all these races from A to Z. From Arcturian Pleiadians to an Alien Z's Species, all saying we are being assisted by all of creation: the Spiritual Hierarchy, angelic realms, ascended masters, our so-called space brothers. You may have heard of The Galactic Federation of Light, leaders such as Ashtar and others, who give messages to mankind.

Just like so-called ghosts they claim to advocate for global unity, inclusion and peace for all, teaching that eventually we will all come together, all religions and beliefs, under one great teacher, an ancient messiah-type figure.

We noticed from our experience, and all down history, dead people and spirit guides all taught these similar things. Notably they also taught the Bible was wrong about Jesus being the Saviour, that we didn't need to be forgiven by Him to attain eternal life in heaven and that, in fact, there was no heaven or hell, just various levels of spiritual planes we could ascend to, or indeed, we could return here on earth by reincarnation, to further our journey towards, "attaining a higher consciousness and spiritual enlightenment."

The significance of Lucifer
We were taught that Lucifer, the Light Bearer, was the only true, good and loving God. One day he will unite the world in peace and then everyone will worship him. Although not all mediums are aware of this teaching it is still taught in top New Age books and websites. It originates from teachings spread in the 1830s by the famous Luciferian Medium, Madam Helena Blavatsky, known as Mother of The New Age Movement.

Spirits and spirit guides told her this information about Lucifer. Material by her and her prodigy Alice Bailey are still taught, especially by The Lucis Trust and other

Theosophy groups. Foster Bailey, husband of Alice, was an author too. He wrote on Freemasonry. So, being a Mason, he believed like Alice, that Lucifer is God.

They all taught the Bible was wrong, especially where the Book of Revelation predicts global chaos in the Last Days, the world uniting to worship and be deceived by the Antichrist, and ultimately Jesus destroying him at the end of the world. If these spirits were liars, we realised this meant Lucifer really is Satan and the Bible and Book of Revelation is true!

<u>Nagging doubts</u>
These famous quotes come to mind, "The greatest trick the Devil ever pulled was convincing the world he didn't exist," wrote Charles Baudelaire.

"The second greatest trick the Devil ever pulled was convincing the world he is the good guy," wrote Ken Ammi.

Like many we did realise that if these spirits are lying, then we *all* are in great danger, as it implies they are not kind spirits under the headship of Lucifer, but evil demons under the dominion of Satan. But, like everyone else, the more we became involved the more we trusted spirits.

At times we would also wonder if channelling could be too dangerous but other, more experienced, mediums would reassure us saying, "Sometimes mischievous spirits will come through. Yes, it's a risk we all take. A hazard of the job, but if you have good karma, like attracts like, so most times only good spirits will visit. We'll teach you how to protect yourselves to stay safe."

Was that good enough? We weren't totally convinced, yet, like everyone else, we were totally captivated, even addicted, so carried on regardless.

Strange phenomena

Things seemed fine for years. We really enjoyed attending and developing but now and then we would hear concerning accounts of problems within the paranormal community. Eventually we heard rumours from various spiritualist churches of mediums running into more serious difficulties, even no longer able to channel spirits safely. Spirits would come through against their will, start to control them, putting them into trances at any time and even becoming verbally and physically abusive and downright violent. Other mediums shared how their so-called spirit guides and dead relatives not only became aggressive, but even told them lies, or attempted to lead them astray.

Spirits attack us

What Hollywood and many others would describe as poltergeist experiences, and other phenomena that can't be explained scientifically, began happening to us too. Spirits violently moved furniture and slammed doors. Electrical appliances switched on and began working even though they weren't plugged into power. Along with us our cats and dogs became deeply alarmed at sudden movements, unearthly loud noises and visual apparitions.

We were both physically attacked by spirits. It felt utterly horrific, like nothing you've ever experienced before. They claimed to be our trusted dead relatives and ascended spirit guides! So why were they doing this to us? My mother was more involved in spirit communication than I was. She was physically thrown around by them. While out shopping, I and others literally saw her being lifted and thrown onto the bonnet of a passing car. One day, while cooking, spirits took over against her will, forcing her into a trance. She was unaware the entire kitchen was being engulfed by flames. Thankfully the fire brigade came and extinguished it before it spread throughout our home.

We were often kept awake at night with intense phenomena. My attention at school and then college was affected. It was terrifying and extremely traumatic. We were literally being terrorised by evil forces. It became a horrendous nightmare for us both. We probably suffered from Post Traumatic Stress Disorder. We endured incredible upheaval in our daily lives.

This hellish paranormal activity became even worse. Visiting our local library we searched through religious and metaphysical encyclopaedias for spiritual help. Once back home we would call out to different gods and entities for help. We even meditated more and practised more yoga, assured by the mediums this would help connect us to higher guides who would evict these lower-level spirits. Although yoga and meditation are so popular today most don't realise that even if you don't feel it, these practices connect you to spirits. This has been known by yogis and those practising New Age, witchcraft and the occult for many generations. We hoped this would connect us with more evolved and benevolent spirit guides, from more ancient star systems.

Although the general public refer to them as "aliens," we felt this was a derogatory term as we believed them, more accurately, to be ascended beings of light. None of our efforts seeking help from them actually worked. In fact circumstances only grew far worse. We wondered why. Could all of these spirits and gods ultimately be evil imposters, pretending to be ghosts and spirit guides? Wasn't there any higher being in the greater cosmos who could help us survive this battle? We felt we were reaching the complete end of our wits.

Psychiatric hospital

My mother asked her doctor for sleeping pills as the spirits constantly harassed her, especially during the night. Tragically the medic didn't believe my mother's account of events and, like many other channellers and occultists being diagnosed as schizophrenic, my mum was admitted into a psychiatric hospital. Along with our family we were completely heartbroken. We sadly remembered hearing of this happening to others involved in channelling spirits and spirit guides.

The turning point

At university I began an Honours Degree in Psychology. I met a Christian woman whom I became friendly with. I shared with her what had happened to my mum and me. She told me about Jesus and the Bible. She said He could help. I thought she was stupid, spiritually unevolved and likely had bad karma, so didn't believe her at first. We had been taught that Jesus was just an ascended master, a great psychic healer and that His mother, the Virgin Mary, had been impregnated by an alien god from a visiting UFO, not the Holy Spirit as the Bible states. We had been told humans were all descended from ancient alien civilisations and the Bible was fraudulent so we should disregard it.

She said a Christian minister with the gift of prophecy would be speaking at a church she knew. That was the hook the Holy Spirit used to draw me along. Being a New Ager I was fascinated by prophecies and predictions, so this really attracted me.

I agreed to go and I really loved it! I was deeply impressed. More importantly I felt a strong spiritual presence that I hadn't ever sensed before. It was so overwhelming, exquisitely beautiful and peaceful. This completely intrigued me, because this "spirit being," or god felt unlike any spirit or spirit guide I'd ever encountered.

People were singing and praying in other tongues. That really fascinated me. They were also praying for healing which also attracted me. I knew something supernatural was taking place and yet they weren't communicating with spirits. So later, travelling back home, many questions ran through my mind.

Spirits threaten to kill me
When I returned home the spirits were furious that I'd been to the Christian church. It was utterly horrendous. Just as they had led to my mum being incarcerated I actually thought they would succeed in killing me. They were enraged that I was drifting out of the occult and heading towards the Lord. I sensed they wanted me dead. They didn't want me sharing our experiences with others! They hate the truth.

I didn't ask Jesus Christ into my life that night at the church but He was definitely on my mind. I wondered if He really is the Son of God. So I prayed to Him. When I shouted the name of Jesus the supernatural attacks instantly stopped and the spirits vanished!

This amazed me. Absolutely nothing we had tried before could stop such attacks! I was so deeply grateful. It felt as if Jesus had saved my life. After all the years of spiritual torture and chaos I felt sure a peace would be finally entering my soul.

While drifting off to sleep I kept thinking of a Romany woman, a fortune teller, who visited our neighbourhood around once a year to read palms. I couldn't understand why she was on my mind.

My salvation
The next morning the doorbell rang. To my great surprise it was the Romany woman! Rather than offering to read my palm like she would usually do, she surprised me by saying, "I've become a Christian. Jesus freed me from spirits, divination and psychic powers. He led me here today, to speak to you. What you saw at the place you visited last night was the truth."

This was all the confirmation I needed. I knew pieces of the jigsaw were finally falling into perfect place. That day I asked the Jesus of the Bible into my heart and life, to become my Saviour. I was extremely thankful and ready to develop a close, personal, lifelong relationship with Him. I repented from everything, turning away from the New Age, spiritualism and anything involving other religions, spiritualities, witchcraft or the occult.

The truth of Christ's existence

I began attending church with my university friend. I soon learned of the academic discipline known as apologetics. I discovered, contrary to popular belief, true science is not incompatible with Christianity at all! Many scholars, including university professors, in various specialist areas like history, archaeology, geology and so on, provide evidence for the authenticity of the Bible, for Biblical creation, and the existence of Biblical historical figures, especially Jesus Christ! He is *not* merely a mythical figure or reincarnation of other pagan, so called, saviour-gods.

In addition apologists provide evidence that the beliefs in other religions, gods, goddesses, spirits, etc. are not based in fact but are indeed false gods, just as the Bible describes, existing to deceive and keep people from salvation in Christ alone.

I was amazed! There really is proof that the Holy Scriptures are true and that everything recorded there about Jesus is factual. More importantly most historians admit there's plenty of evidence that Jesus really did live, die on the cross for our sins and rise again. Absolutely no one in the entire history of the world ever did that!

Therefore He really is the Saviour! It's true, you really *do* need to come to Him for forgiveness, to avoid hell, and gain eternal life in heaven. I certainly never thought I would become a Christian, but as a truth seeker I could not deny the clear evidence.

Like most people, when you hear the truth regarding something as significant as this, you must go where the truth leads you. "Jesus answered, 'I am the way and the truth and the life. No one comes to the Father except through me.'" John 14:6. Once you have heard this vital and unforgettable truth, you cannot unhear it. As all philosophers and great scholars will agree it's one of the top answers concerning the purpose and meaning of life and the universe.

To discover Jesus really is the God that we *all* need in our lives and eternities, is the *most* important fact you will ever hear. So, I humbly ask you to take time to really think this over. Where does Jesus stand in your life? Do you actually know Him, and do you know and daily walk with Him intimately? You can! He is not distant, angry and uncaring. He loves you so much He died for your sins on Calvary's cross, so you can be restored to our Heavenly Father, the Creator.

He is knocking at the door of your heart, even right now! In the very last book of the Bible, Jesus says to you, "Behold, I stand at the door and knock. If anyone hears My voice and opens the door, I will come in to him..." Revelation 3:20. If you think you have gone too far to be forgiven, consider the Apostle Paul. Before he came to Jesus, he was a killer, murdering Christians. No one has to perish. "The Lord is ... not willing that any should perish, but that all should come to repentance," 2 Peter 3:9.

Truths about ghosts and spirit guides
When I became a Christian I started to read the Bible. I felt as if God was answering my questions on what had happened. I would be thinking or praying over something then open the Bible and there was the explanation!

"Familiar spirits," the term used in the King James Version of the Bible, describes in Hebrew, the original language of the Old Testament, evil spirits. So where mediums are said to have "familiar spirits," this actually means evil spirits or demons, not dead people!

Familiar spirits and divination spirits are all evil demons, also known as fallen angels. "There shall not be found among you any one that makes his son or his daughter to pass through the fire, or that uses divination, or an observer of times, or an enchanter, or a witch, or a charmer, or a consulter with familiar spirits, or a wizard, or a necromancer. For all that do these things are an abomination unto the Lord..." Deuteronomy 18:10-12.

Such spirit beings once existed in heaven as good angels worshipping God, but sinned becoming fallen angels that God cast from heaven. Therefore these evil demons have existed for so long, retaining knowledge of our families and historical figures down the generations. They can easily disguise their evil form to morph, mimic our dead relatives and shape-shift into the appearance of alien spirit guides, angels, goddesses and so on.

"And no wonder, for Satan himself masquerades as an angel of light. It is not surprising, then, if his servants also masquerade as servants of righteousness..." 2 Corinthians 11:14-15.

Those so called dead people and spirit guides had offered guidance and kindness to us for years. It's obvious they'd actually deceived us and been evil all along.

You might be wondering, "So, if these are imposters, where are the true ghosts?" There are no ghosts. The Bible shows that it's impossible for souls of the dead to become earthbound, visit or watch over us. Instead, upon death, every soul will go to heaven or hell for eternity. "And as it is appointed unto men once to die, but after this the judgment." Hebrews 9:27.

Being supernatural, demons can give you powerful experiences and dreams, convincing you of past lives and reincarnation, or astral projection, convincing you of meeting goddesses, visiting aliens and dead people on UFOs, other galaxies or so-called parallel timelines. However, these spirits leave, their deceptive lies are exposed; these experiences, nightmares and sleep paralysis stop when the contacted person receives deliverance from Jesus.

In a parable where Jesus speaks of the impossibility of travelling between heaven, hell and earth to speak with relatives, He taught that Abraham said, "...between us and you a great chasm has been set in place, so that those who want to go from here to you cannot, nor can anyone cross over from there to us." Luke 16:26.

In the oft-cited case of The Witch of Endor, the King James Bible states she had a "familiar spirit," and, as I said, in Biblical Hebrew this means an evil demon. Although she was consulted by Saul to summon the spirit of the prophet Samuel, it was a demon that rose and impersonated him. No medium or demon can summon dead people.

Author, Rev. Mark Hunnemann, a world expert on debunking "ghosts," who like myself, has spent many years helping people to get freed from demonic attack, kindly wrote the following for me,

"The notion of earthbound spirits or ghosts is contrary to a Biblical worldview. Namely, it's contrary to the Biblical view of the nature of God, the Biblical view of our purpose in life, the nature of reality, the Biblical view of history, incompatible with a basis for morality, contrary to the essential traits of being human, and is contrary to what the Bible teaches about what happens when we die. In a word, earthbound spirits is profoundly antithetical to Biblical worldview.

Perhaps worst of all the notion of earthbound spirits diminishes one's perception of their need of salvation, as well as the perfection of the finished work of Christ on the cross.

The only conclusion regarding ghosts that is compatible with scripture, a Biblical worldview and my own experience, is that ghosts are demons."

Author, Dana Emanuel, a former ghost hunter and world expert on debunking "ghosts," who, like myself, spent many years helping people to get freed from demonic attack, kindly wrote the following,

"These spirits also tell people they can repent and receive Christ as Saviour, *after* death, which is not Biblical, '...as it is appointed to men once to die, but after this the judgment,' Hebrews 9:27."

Dana also listed more similarities of ghosts and alien spirit guides, to emphasise their similar behaviour and intentions, showing they are all demons in disguise.

- They all cause "paranormal" activity.
- They all have the ability to communicate with humans telepathically.
- They all have the ability to appear out of nowhere, morph, cloak and disappear suddenly.
- They are all involved in sleep paralysis, night terrors, and "out of body" experiences.
- There are often light anomalies involved with them.
- They have been known to "teach people about Jesus," but the Jesus they describe does not line up with the true Jesus of the Bible. It's very telling that they find it very important to "change" who we think Jesus is!
- They ALL flee when commanded to, in the name of Jesus!

More evidence that ghosts and spirit guides are evil impostors

Whether a medium, guru, any type of channeller, priest or even Christian minister speaks with entities claiming to be, for example, ghosts, aliens, angels, goddesses, fairies, spirits of dead Nephilim, prophets, saints or anyone from the Bible, run from them! Indeed, any being, even so-called Big Foot, or *any* other entity, or strange creature, remember, they share a few other critically telling points in common.

Whether they contact people audibly, visually or telepathically, countless people worldwide report they *all* can lie, attack, cause you temporary paralysis and so on. Also they become irritated or distraught at the mention of the cross, the blood, and name of Jesus Christ of Nazareth, the true Messiah.

If you command them to leave in Jesus' name they vanish.

This scenario repeats over and over proving, just as the Bible shows, they are *all* evil deceptive demons masquerading as various identities!

Eddie Bennett and Alan Brooks were former alien contactees and UFO cult members. Eddie shared with me how the UFO group members had to take oaths to renounce Jesus Christ at the request of their "alien" contacts! It's a red flag that the only one they wanted them to renounce was Jesus! No wonder they flee at the mention of His name! Alan shared a similar testimony to many, that he was freed from alien abduction experiences when he received deliverance from Christ.

All such entities, including the so called Galactic Federation of Light, are actually a Demonic Hierarchy of Lies. As it says in Ephesians 6:12, "For our struggle is not against flesh and blood, but against the rulers, against the authorities, against the powers of this dark world and against the spiritual forces of wickedness in high places."

The Bible says even some of the church will be deceived in the end times. When more so-called aliens and ghosts appear globally, the media and even church will run with it, helping deceive the entire world. This is all part of the End Times spiritual strong delusion, mentioned in 2 Thessalonians 2:11.

Destroying New Age books
I joined my friend's church and, at the advice of the minister and others, burned my many books and magazines on the New Age, spiritualism and so on. Throughout the

Bible, when people repented of such things, they burned their books and paraphernalia, severing ties with the occult and making a clean start.

My mother's salvation

I shared everything with my mother. She was sceptical at first, then said she wasn't surprised and asked to come to church. The psychiatric hospital allowed me to take her. Soon after she also asked Jesus to become her Saviour, repenting of the occult. I was overjoyed!

Unthinkable tragedy strikes: My mother's suicide

Already suffering from stress and depression because spiritual harassment continued, I realised I would probably endure further spiritual attack and could end up in a psychiatric hospital like my mum. After a while she was released. But a far worse tragedy struck.

Once back home she was again tormented by spirits. This was hardly surprising as they'd not been evicted yet. Our pastor didn't have experience of casting spirits out and thought because we were now Christians there couldn't be any. But those spirits still harassed me in the home I lived in with my husband and child. They continued to terrorise my mother in her home too.

To my utter shock and dismay she committed suicide. My own dear mother took her life! I feel because our pastor wouldn't visit to cleanse her home she lost hope. I truly believe if the church had cast the demons out my mother would still be alive. I've heard countless similar stories since 1996. This highlights how crucial it is the church obeys the Bible and casts demons out in Jesus name, just as the disciples did in the New Testament.

Her suicide was beyond my deepest fears and imagination. And yet I remembered when one of her brothers and her spiritualist aunt were present in our home during paranormal disturbance. Each visited on different occasions during activity and in abject horror shouted the same thing: that this could lead to our suicides unless we got help! They were absolutely right. I was completely devastated. I feared this could soon happen to me too. My life was going downhill. And fast!

Deliver us from evil
Even although I had burned all occult books I was still experiencing the same demonic attacks I'd experienced for years. I would feel a presence pin me down, like a heavy lead weight crushing my chest, invisible hands trying to strangle me. I would splutter and choke. It felt like I was being paralysed and the presence of evil was strong. I had tried to pray but couldn't speak. Eventually, I'd manage to shout Jesus' name. The demons left but there was only temporary relief, until the next time. Unknown to me then this is a classic example Christians report of demonic attack! Thankfully it ends when we receive full deliverance from Jesus, as I was soon to gratefully discover.

My deliverance and road to restoration
Just as they had led to my mother's suicide, I knew spirits wanted me dead. They didn't want me sharing our experiences to help others!

I again shared this with our pastor, but he argued Christians can't have demons in their home or body. Like many churches he assumed the moment you become a Christian demons *automatically* just leave, without being literally cast out. This logic suggests the moment someone becomes a Christian they'll receive automatic healing in their body, but that's not often true. Usually they need to pray or have a minister pray with them for healing.

He advised my husband to admit me to the psychiatric hospital even although he knew about my mother's time there and suicide. Thankfully my husband knew it was spiritual and not a mental health issue.

We looked for a helpful church; it was a long search! Eventually we found one that *did* believe in casting demons out of Christian and non-Christian people and homes, just as the Bible shows. "And when he had called unto him his twelve disciples, he gave them power against unclean spirits, to cast them out, and to heal all manner of sickness and all manner of disease," Matthew 10:1.

Jesus and the apostles healed the sick and cast demons out of anyone who needed help. They never specified it was only non-Christians who need physical healing or freeing from spirits! The Lord warned His people throughout the Bible to avoid witchcraft, false gods etc. He knew these cause our souls to be defiled by evil spirits. "Regard not them that have familiar spirits, neither seek after wizards, to be defiled by them: I am the LORD your God," Leviticus 19:31. Jesus came to set the captives free!

To cast demons out of me and our home the pastor used no rituals, religious icons or paraphernalia. Just using faith in the Name, cross and blood of Jesus Christ is enough to command them to leave in Jesus' name. As the Bible says, at Calvary's cross, "...having disarmed principalities and powers, He made a show of them openly, triumphing over them in it," Colossians 2:15. The demons were also cast from my late mother's home so I sold it with a clear conscience.

Most wouldn't be surprised if demons were cast from a former witch, or Satanist, so it's no surprise they were cast out of me, a former spiritualist. There's no difference! The apostle Paul cast a demon out of this psychic woman. "Once when we were going to the place of prayer, we were met by a female slave possessed with a spirit of divination by which she predicted the future. She earned a great deal of money for her owners by fortune-telling." Acts 16:16-18.

After the pastor cast demons out of me and our home, there were no more physical attacks, sleep paralysis or visits from "dead family or alien spirit guides."

Since 1997 I have heard countless similar testimonies from Christians worldwide who struggled to find a church that believed they needed such help. Tragically many of them, like my mum, were committed into psychiatric hospitals or became suicidal. Some did commit suicide and their loved ones told me the story. Thankfully, like me, many of them found a church or Christian friend who cast the demons out and they finally found peace. Many were also healed as those involved in the occult can commonly be plagued with health problems.

Transformation
My entire life and behaviour changed. My whole mindset and outlook even changed. More and more layers of deception were lifted from me. That was in 1996. Since then not once has any spirit appeared pretending to be my dead relative, spirit guide and so on! Dreams of world domination by aliens ended. Clearly they realise I know the

truth of their real demonic identity so they don't even try to deceive me with their diabolical lies and deceptive appearances anymore.

One of the first scriptures that encouraged me as a new Christian was, "You will not fear the terror of night..." Psalm 91:5. On reading it I felt the Lord was assuring me I would no longer be attacked spiritually, especially in the night.

I frequently meet or hear from Christians online who came from different religions, or are former psychic mediums, healers, pagans, Wiccans, witches, shamans, Satanists and so on.

Interestingly they all report similar things: they discovered their so-called dead relatives, spirit guides, gods or goddesses were actually evil demons but upon saying the name of Jesus Christ at them these demonic spirits left. They will tend to deny the Incarnation of Jesus, that He died for our sins on the cross and that His powerful blood defeats sin and them. They react to such truths with screaming, lashing out then disappearing quickly. We sometimes see such reactions when cleansing homes harassed by so called "ghosts," and so on.

These precious people were set free from being demonised and from any further demonic attack, curses or illnesses placed upon them after asking Christ into their hearts and receiving spiritual freedom, when deliverance ministers cast those demons from their presence. Demons were not just temporarily gone but gone forever never to return!

"Dear friends, do not believe every spirit, but test the spirits to see whether they are from God, because many false prophets have gone out into the world. This is how you can recognize the Spirit of God: Every spirit that acknowledges that Jesus Christ has come in the flesh is from God, but every spirit that does not acknowledge Jesus is not from God. This is the spirit of the antichrist, which you have heard is coming and even now is already in the world." 1 John 4:1-3.

Even logical deduction shows none of this could be sheer coincidence, especially considering everything else shared here. In 2 Thessalonians 2:9, the Bible mentions that Satan works with all power and signs and lying wonders.

Instead of being fearful of evil spirits because of my past experience, Christ enabled me to overcome and then to help people suffering from such harassment, even cleansing their homes, casting those demons out, in the name of Jesus. He has radically changed me and given me boldness. I don't fear those things anymore. Now I can help others by his love and power, bringing people to faith and freedom; even people who have come out of the darkest types of Satanism.

"He has delivered us from the power of darkness and brought us into the kingdom of the Son He loves, in whom we have redemption through His blood, the forgiveness of sins." Colossians 1:13-14.

Jesus has truly done a work of transformation in my life. For years I thought I could never experience lasting happiness and peace in my life. Today I can honestly say that I do.

"The cords of death entangled me, the torrents of destruction overwhelmed me...in my distress I called to the Lord. I cried to my God for help. From His temple He heard my voice..." Psalm 18:4, 6.

The Holy Spirit's guidance
The Bible explains the Lord Himself wants to guide and teach you through the Holy Spirit. At my water baptism, by revelation from the Holy Spirit, the pastor felt led to give me the scripture, "Call to me and I will answer you and tell you great and unsearchable things you do not know," Jeremiah 33:3. Since 1996 that very verse has been given by the Holy Spirit to me many times by Christians who know nothing about me. It has been accurate. The Lord continues to graciously guide and teach me, revealing things through reading the Bible and prayer.

So, ask God, the Creator, speak to Him, not spirits or any type of New Age divination. You can receive direction from the Holy Spirit of Almighty God too! The Bible tells us everything He wants us to know and about the future. We don't need to seek revelation from any other spiritual source.

New Age and occult infiltrating the church worldwide
Just as the Bible predicts, "The Spirit clearly says that in the last days, some will depart from the faith, giving heed to deceiving spirits and doctrines taught by demons." 1 Timothy 4:1. Not only does this affect your faith, as the Bible shows, you and your family will be cursed by such demons, even with ill health.

"For false Christs and false prophets shall rise, and shall show signs and wonders, to deceive, if it were possible, even the elect." Mark 13:22.

I constantly hear of Christians trying New Age remedies or claiming they were contacted by the dead spirit of a revivalist preacher, Biblical prophet or people from the great cloud of witnesses in Hebrews 12. Some even say they receive revelation from the elders and living creatures that surround God's throne in heaven, Revelation 4. Again there is nothing in the Bible that says this is God's will, or even possible. What's more if they repent and the lying demons are evicted such experiences stop!

Some Christians refer to energies from the universe sending vibes and so on, not discerning such are counterfeit "energies" from evil demons, physically felt counterfeit anointings. Even deliverance ministers, instead of simply praying in Jesus name to evict demons, are using occult methods like shamanic sage burning, pouring salt and so on.

Sadly most ministers fail to warn their churches about such things and the people don't read their Bibles like the Bereans, checking if latest fads line up with scripture or are demonic lies and curses. "...My people are destroyed from lack of knowledge." Hosea 4:6. Various areas can be destroyed: your family, health, even your life.

<u>My story's relevance for you</u>
Although at first you might feel my story and paranormal experience is irrelevant to you, I'm sure you recognise it contains truths about Jesus and your own eternal soul that are crucial to take heed of.

Remember that I shared that there is indisputable evidence from historical, archaeological and geological records which apologists teach, to verify the Bible and the existence and teachings of Jesus? Thus, the Bible being true, everything Jesus said and did being true, then it is also true that we all need Him. Including you.

It is therefore, clearly, also true that every other religion and spirit is indeed deceptive - their purpose being to convince you they are real, to cause you to doubt the truth about Christ and the Bible, and divert your attention away from salvation in Him. They seduce you to plummet into the most deceptive of all rabbit holes to be consumed with their endless lies. So these are indeed false gods, or evil demons, as the Bible explains. They follow the direction of their master, the greatest deceiver of all time, Satan, "...the father of lies." John 8:44.

If you have never asked Jesus into your life to become your Saviour, to forgive and cleanse you, and give you a new start in life, please do so now. The Holy Spirit will help guide you and develop a close, personal relationship with our loving Heavenly Father for the rest of your life. Saved from hell, you will experience the peace and joy of heaven for all eternity, once your life on earth ends.

It's my sincere desire this transformative testimony brings you, your friends or loved ones hope and encouragement. If Jesus Christ could rescue me from such a deep, dark pit He can do the same for you! Whatever problem you are facing, He can help and empower you to overcome it. He can bring you more victory and breakthroughs than you thought possible.

"Now to Him who is able to do immeasurably more than all we ask or imagine, according to His power that is at work within us, to Him be glory in the church and in Christ Jesus throughout all generations, forever and ever! Amen," Ephesians 3:20-21.

He still does miracles in our modern world today. Nothing is impossible with God! If you are in old age He will remain by your side even as you pass through the shadow of death to enter eternity with Him.

Equipping you to help others
As I mentioned above, few people talk about suffering spiritual problems, fearing others' reactions or being diagnosed as mentally ill. I hope what I have written helps you share evidence that these dangerous experiences are demonic and to encourage people to find lasting freedom, from being demonised, from attacks, curses and illnesses demons placed upon them. Instead they can be blessed by peace and joy from the merciful and loving Saviour, Jesus Christ.

"And these signs shall follow them that believe; in my name shall they cast out devils; they shall speak with new tongues; they shall take up serpents; and if they drink any deadly thing, it shall not hurt them; they shall lay hands on the sick, and they shall recover," Mark 16:17-18.

People can defeat spirits and be freed permanently, having them cast out by the authority and power in the mention of Jesus name, His cross and blood. They can continue to walk in such freedom by developing a close and accountable relationship with Him.

As Jesus taught, "The Spirit of the Lord is upon me, because He has anointed me to preach the gospel to the poor; He has sent me to heal the broken hearted, to preach deliverance to the captives ..." Luke 4:18.

So, do not be afraid. "You, dear children, are from God and have overcome them, because greater is He that is in you, than he that is in the world." 1 John 4:4.

<u>Concluding words</u>
In these troubled times more adults, teenagers and children are turning to the occult whether seeking answers or entertainment. It's so easy to access online ghost, Ouija and tarot apps, Wicca spells for health and relationships, and so on. Such practices can now be easily blended by anyone, producing a toxic spiritual cocktail. Disney, Hollywood, the general media, even education and science promote avenues of spiritual darkness, making it all seem beneficial.

Since 2008 I've been honoured to serve in Christian ministry. It's been a great honour to be a guest speaker in venues, conferences and youth groups across the UK and abroad, on satellite TV or radio channels around the world and to host my own show *The Supernatural with Laura Maxwell*, on Eternal Radio, during which my guests and I share our true stories or teach about dangers of the New Age, the occult, etc. People worldwide continue to contact me requesting help, seeking answers or to share their similar testimonies with me, which I sometimes post on my blog. Some of them I also interview for podcasts, many of which can be viewed on my YouTube channel and other social media. These and blog articles by myself and others could be useful to share with your family or friends if they are experiencing what we once did. If my story or any of my work has touched you or them, please send me a message. I'd love to hear from you! See "Acknowledgements and Further Information" at the end of this book.

Liam's story

Liam fell so low but Jesus lifted him up high.

Sixteen years ago I hit rock bottom.

Three prison sentences, two suicide attempts, sixteen years of drug addiction. I needed help.

I ended up going to a drug treatment centre that was run by Christians but it didn't mean anything to me.

After a while I noticed that the staff had something different about them. A love, joy and a peace in their lives and I wanted to know how.

So I asked them.

They told me it was because of their relationship with Jesus.

So I started to go to church with them. I started to listen. I started to ask questions.

There wasn't a big moment for me but the more I went, the more I pursued it, the more peace I felt and the more I accepted myself.

I'm sixteen years drug-free now. I'm happily married. I have four beautiful children and I love the life that I have.

The good news is no matter who you are and where you've been, today Jesus can change your life just like he changed mine.

Lisa's story

Ten-year-old Lisa suffered immeasurable pain following her parents' breakup but she had been noticed sitting behind a pillar in a church; the reason for her searching was a gift of God to her. She is now a new creation.

Was I converted at the age of twelve, or was it earlier? Both, I think, because in my tenth year, in the wake of my mother taking her three children away with her as she left my father, the pain in my soul was so acute that, nearly sixty years later, I still tear up remembering.

And yet, it was that pain which opened up the door of faith for me. Where did that chink of light come from? Was it a fleeting memory of time spent over several very early years in Sunday school? Perhaps. My parents had belonged to churches once, but we did not attend, and had the family not been torn apart I certainly was destined for a comfortable existence without the thought of gods of any kind.

I was the eldest child, and the first of our small severed family to find faith. It happened thus....

My mother put me into a fee-paying Roman Catholic preparatory school, where for my last year before the then ten-plus examination I discovered love in the special attention of a godly Christian teacher there. I can't remember her name, but I'll know her when we meet in Heaven. She took this new, non-Catholic, much-traumatised young girl under her wing and brought me not merely back to life but also set me on the road to finding life.

Strangely, although I was exempt from RE lessons I stayed in for them, and listened, and took to walking to school with my hand in Father God's. Father God took over from my dad I think, but it was more than that. It was comforting to hold God's hand and talk to Him. "Dear God, if you're there, please show me," I would pray.

As I walked I wanted to be closer to my strange, silent friend and so I started visiting my local church on Sunday mornings. Nowadays parents wouldn't let their children walk alone as much as I did but back then we walked everywhere without fear.

In the Sunday services at my nearest Church of England parish church I would find a seat behind a pillar. I would stay there but not for the whole of each service, only up to the sermon as I had been told that sermons were boring. I would then quietly stand up and make my way to the ancient door. I would quietly push the latch to open it and slip out into the sunlight and make my way home. This behaviour meant that I was never stopped or greeted at the end of that lively, evangelical Anglican church service.

When I was aged twelve my mother told me that being religious was a phase that some girls go through and that I would grow out of it. I thought carefully about this and was quite prepared to do so, partly because I by then started wondering what relevance Jesus might have - they talked about him at school and in church and yet it all sounded most improbable. My mind had already taken a scientific streak and all this talk of resurrection felt, well, distant - there was to be no more holding hands with a dead, or risen, saviour man.

I made a pledge - I would give it three more months of going to church and then, if God had not shown me Jesus was real, I would stop; I would grow out of it and let my mother's cynicism of the world take root. That felt quite okay. So I prayed. I prayed, "Dear God, if Jesus is relevant, show me, please. And do it within the next three months. Or I will stop thinking about all this."

Nothing changed for maybe ten weeks until one night it struck me that if I wanted God to show me something I should be willing to make some effort to find out. And so on the next Sunday I stayed in my seat behind the pillar longer than usual and I heard the sermon. At the end of the service I was still there and able for the first time to mill around at the back with others.

"Would you like that book, love?" asked a middle-aged lady who had noticed me standing awkwardly by the bookstall. I was looking at a brightly coloured version of the classic book that Michael Green had written for teenagers called "Man Alive!" I didn't speak, I just nodded. She put some money in the tin and handed me the book. I walked home eager to begin it.

Nowadays I look at copies of that book and see all sorts of problems with it - tiny typeface, non-inclusive language, yellowed pages, didactic teaching. It's not a book that I could now hand to someone who might be asking questions. Yet back then I read it to the centre pages where the evidence for the resurrection is laid out well; the doubts in my mind about that dropped into the corners of my mind in such a way that I remember closing the book, turning to the window in my bedroom where the light was streaming in, and feeling faith. The faith poured into me. I knew. I could believe.

Later that week a neighbour stopped me on the path. "You're a very happy bunny this week, child - what's happened to you?" she asked. I didn't say. I couldn't say - perhaps especially when my mother asked a similar question. It was weeks before I had the language to describe it - by which time a godly single Pathfinder teacher called Mavis had picked me up and put me in her class at church, and I was learning who I really was in Christ.

It was years later that my mother joined the Quakers and then further years before my sister was converted too. And then, ten years and six house-moves later, I learned the basis for the fact that despite everything and all the lonely distances from the church where I found faith, I had remained a Christian.

Mavis had discovered where I was living - in digs at Manchester University - and passed the address on to the wife of the parson in their church. Her name was Mrs Person (which is probably why I do still remember that) but I did not remember her. However she remembered me as for the past ten years, "Every Saturday or other Saturday when I sit down to pray for people" she said in her letter, she thought of, "The small girl who used to sit behind the pillar at the back, and left before the end" and she had prayed for me. She wrote that she was glad to have learned that I was well, had become a Christian and was still a child of God.

Since then my stories of conversion are many and I'm still en route to it, I think. I've tried to unbelieve quite often -

Christianity is most confusing sometimes - and been disillusioned on occasions for good reason. Yet I know, with all that I now am, that I'm the lucky one. The searing schism in my family that set me searching was a gift of God to me. Because of it I am a new creation and my heart is full of gratitude and faith. Prayers that once felt contradictory or impossible, or highly unlikely - prayers sent up at different times within my life - have all been "followed up" amazingly, after often many years.

Now, as a serving priest, I often look at the children in my churches and remember how it felt, and what my thoughts were way back then.

I pray for them all.

Mandy's story

Brought up in the Sikh religion, Mandy wasn't looking for Jesus but He revealed Himself to her during a period of turmoil in her life.

A few weeks ago I was baptised with my two children. It was the most amazing day! It actually ended up being the best day of my life.

Growing up my faith looked a lot different to what it looks like now. I was brought up in the Sikh religion; I was brought up to believe in one god and I felt from a young age that I definitely had a relationship with God, but I didn't know Jesus. The difference between then and now is that I now have a relationship with God through Jesus Christ and that's the big difference.

I became a Christian when I was forty-three. That was about three years ago. Jesus Christ actually revealed himself to me. I wasn't looking for Jesus, I didn't know of Jesus, I didn't grow up with Jesus coming from a Sikh background but at the time I was going through the most turbulent time of my life and my mind was in complete and utter turmoil. That was the moment that Jesus chose to reveal himself to me.

In our bedroom at the time we didn't have curtains. We have a tree in our back garden so often at night I would look out of the window and at the leaves on the tree. This particular night at about three o'clock in the morning when I was at my most despairing I reached out to my father. He had passed away when I was twelve years old. I said, "Dad, please help." My vision instantly changed from the leaves to

102

the cross formed by the frame on the window. Instantly. It was involuntarily as well. I thought, "Why has my focus just changed, just at that moment that I asked for help?"

From that moment on everything else changed.

I started to go to church and look for more answers and learn more about Jesus.

I would sit in the front row and listen to the vicar Dave [Johnson, Christ Church, Chislehurst]. There always seemed to be a message for me. I know people say that but there always seemed to be a message for me for that day as to how I was feeling. I started to speak to more people. I was handed a Bible. I procrastinated over the Bible for some time, wondering where I was going to start but a friend said to me, "Just pick it up and start reading from the first page." So one night at about eleven o'clock, everyone had gone to sleep, I put a little torch on and I opened the Bible and I started to read the first page. I read the first few pages then put it down. The moment I put it down I experienced this warm feeling that just grew throughout my entire body. It was the first time that I think I had ever experienced the love of Jesus Christ.

I've been a Christian now for three years and what I have realised is that becoming a Christian doesn't mean that life is going to be perfect but what is does mean is that when you are having a turbulent time you can turn to Jesus. Even in your times of joy you will have Jesus with you and that really has transformed my life - knowing that Jesus Christ is there walking with me and my family.

Marion's story

Conversion - a continuing journey.

Dramatic conversions like that of St Paul on the way to Damascus can be likened to the crashing and roar of a wave as it reaches the seashore. That event, although attracting all the attention, is neither the beginning nor the end of the motion of the water. It is simply the event that we see and hear. The wave originated way out at sea, and the consequences of that wave lie in the future.

When I was about thirteen in 1955 I was asked whether or not I had been converted. The question confused me. I had been attending the local Anglican church since I joined the nursery class of the Sunday School at four years old and had been going to Evensong with the family ever since on a Sunday evening. In addition my mother helped me read a passage of Scripture every night with Scripture Union notes to go with it, according to the age I was at the time. "Conversion" was more or less a new term that arrived at the same time as a new vicar who was very evangelical. I was also asked if I had a "spiritual birthday." It reminds me of my young great-nephew who was brought up in a Baptist church. When a visiting preacher came and asked those who wanted to be committed to Christ to come to the front of the church, he went up. When asked about it afterwards by his parents, he said that no one else had gone up so he went as he felt sorry for the preacher. He has since gone on to study Law and is "keeping an open mind" regarding religion.

Years later, after leaving home in 1967 and after many different experiences of life, including the long-term illness of my mother, I found myself in Bristol looking for a church in which to worship. I tried a Methodist church, a high Church of England, a cathedral, but still felt unsatisfied. What they taught was all so different. Sometimes there were contradictory doctrines in the same congregation. I had questions and I wanted real answers. The Roman Catholic church claimed to have the truth so I went to the local Catholic church and asked for instruction. "I am a confirmed, convinced Anglican," I said, "but I want to know more." I wanted to know the meaning of life. I also needed a lot of personal help, but could not bear to accept it until I could trust the Catholics. What if they preached a doctrine which I could not accept?

Happily, the theology of the Catholic church captivated me. It made sense. God was so much greater and omnipotent and so much holier than I had experienced elsewhere, that all else fitted in within this new context. I fell in love with this church and its theology - and with Christ, all over again. Was this a conversion? I rejected the term. I was not turning away from anything. It was the faith that I had found in the Anglican church which had led me to this point and this new development.

That was just the beginning. I had to get used to a whole new set of customs and a very different congregation from the ones of which I had previously been a part. The parish simply did not seem "English" in the way I was used to. This was in 1969, when parishes were still struggling to put into practice the changes of Vatican II. Many of the hymns were different and the style of music was often strange to me. There was little reference, let alone sense of responsibility, to topics of national interest or concern. It was as if it was not really part of the thinking of the congregation.

So this "conversion" meant a rethinking of mental and cultural patterns, and a real change in the way that I thought. There was a lot of rearrangement of my assumptions regarding Catholics in general: many prejudices were still rife in my mind. It meant learning to see the world in a different perspective. It led to reviewing my lifestyle and my job.

I was then working in the Civil Service in an office-based environment. It became clear to me that I was being called to work for greater unity and understanding between the different Christian denominations in the ecumenical movement. To do this I needed to be better qualified. I resigned from my job and was accepted to study Theology at Bristol University. I went on to complete the postgraduate diploma in Pastoral Theology at Heythrop College, then in London. One way or another I was engaged in this ministry for over twenty years but that is another story.

Over the years I went on many Jesuit-run retreats and gradually began to integrate into my being the wonders of a personal relationship with Christ, lived out in the secular world as well as in the church structures. Was this at last the real process of conversion, gradually transforming my life?

"Conversion" as such surely strictly refers to an event where someone changes from one way of life which is broadly against the will of God, to accepting and following the will of God in their life to the best of their ability, trusting wholly in God to provide the help and the means to do this. But this decision must be made over and over again, at different times in our life and in different circumstances.

The decision must be made at all levels of our being. Sometimes the deepest decision comes first, and then has to be ratified at every level of our inner and outer life, over many years. Sometimes it may begin with a seemingly quite minor decision - like my grandmother who decided upon getting married that she would always try to continue to attend the chapel services and did so - and then it gradually deepens to become the bedrock of a person's life.

Although real conversion depends on a decision, it also needs to be lived out in the everyday decisions of our own particular circumstances. And it needs time to take in. St Paul himself went off to Tarsus and spent some years thinking out the implications of what had happened to him. People recently converted need gentle handling. St Ignatius' warning about noting the end of a period of consolation is important because it is then, when still in a heightened state of consciousness, that rogue ideas can creep in. How many sects have been founded after what was probably a genuine conversion experience?

But conversion can never be dissociated from mission. A personal experience of conversion is, of course, a great gift to the individual concerned, but it is also a gift to the church at large and the world around us. How this works out in practice is as individual as the conversion experience.

Conversion is really about the growth of a relationship with our Trinitarian God. Like marriage this is different for every person. Sometimes it starts off with a friendship which gradually develops. Other times there is a sudden and unexpected "falling in love," which seems to short-circuit many of the other stages of getting to know someone. These are usually negotiated later in time. In an arranged marriage the relationship may grow and develop into mature love over many years. Relationships have their own individual journeys. But the relationship with God is always dependent on God's initiative and the person's response of "yes" or "no" or "not yet." Conversion events may simply mark these decisions.

I ran a Rite of Christian Initiation of Adults group for several years. Those who attended came for a variety of reasons. Many came because they were preparing for marriage to a Catholic. Others because they had experienced deep trauma in their lives and were looking for meaning which was not found elsewhere. One person in a group I was running came because he had been asked to be a godparent to his expected nephew and had rarely been to church even though he had been baptised himself. Being confirmed was a requirement in Poland, where the baptism was to take place.

It is intensely moving to see faith growing in people over the weeks and months. It is also inspirational to see the difference in them as they begin to receive the sacraments - if they do. Sadly some appear to lapse quite soon afterwards. Others progress into being faithful and valued members of the church.

The sacramental life of the church is vital and nourishes us at every stage of the way. But the actual occasions of receiving the sacraments, especially that of baptism, does not always coincide in time with actual conversion experiences. When they do the effect is very powerful. The essential strength and effect of, say, infant baptism cannot be assessed but can be considered the very first step of an ultimate transformation.

I prefer the word "transformation" to "conversion" and would apply it to the whole of a life. We are too complex to be "converted" in one moment of time or one special event. Of course these really significant events happen. They "convert" us from what and who we are at the time into a new direction. But I would prefer to say they are significant landmarks on a continuing journey, building on the past which brought us to this point, and looking to the future where we move on to discover new truths.

All this comes under the term of "conversion." But conversion is not the best word to use. I would prefer to call it a growing transformation flowing from decisions made at very different times. The dramatic events are what draw the attention; the real work carries on for years beforehand and a lifetime afterwards. "Transformation" covers the whole process, including those special events which break straight into ordinary time and ordinary lifestyles. We need them - oh yes! But we need also to look at what led up to these events and what follows afterwards.

Life after conversion

The first few years after a specific conversion moment are usually special. The new energy releases many good thoughts and actions and may set the path for many years ahead. But what happens after, say, twenty or thirty years for those who had such an experience when comparatively young?

It may be that some enter a period of great dryness. Consolations seem to be a far-off dream. The realities of life press in on all sides. Prayer may be reduced to a mere, "Lord, have mercy on me," with perhaps an occasional moment of grace which spurs us on during the harsh way we are encountering. This can be a time for pondering all that has happened and all we have done since the dramatic moment of our "conversion." It may be a chance to explore more rationally other ways of thinking and to listen more closely to those who hold different views. If we persevere we may come to a deeper and more solid and integrated faith than the faith that propelled us into activity in earlier years, however fruitful such activity turned out to be. Now may be the time to pray the prayer recommended to me by Michael Ivens SJ in a conversation many years ago: "Pray to the Holy Spirit to show you now, how to respond to the graces of then."

So we plod on and, like the tide which gradually begins to return to the emptied bay of a river estuary, so the dry reeds of our life begin to soften and soak up the life-giving water once more. New ways of service may gently grow in our lives. We may learn to appreciate more our family and friends. Spiritual conversation with friends may provide much support. New, quieter ways of mission open up.

It is a long journey and seems especially so when the active years come to an end. Now is the time to reassess and to believe that we are not abandoned. The Lord has been good to us and will continue to sustain us in the future. It is no time to give up, even though our prayer and service take a very different form as age and infirmity take their toll. We may be a long way from our conversion experience but we are closer than ever to the crucified and risen Lord.

There will be times also when we look back in awe and gratitude at the life we have led and the evidence of God's providence and the work of the Holy Spirit which are apparent throughout. We may experience a great tenderness as we finally enter and embrace a more restricted lifestyle as the exigencies of illness and age make themselves obvious. This is when conversion is seen as a part - even though a most important part - of a lifetime of transformation. We await the final completion of the whole conversion process as we prepare to pass at last into the heart of Christ and so into the beating and living heart of the Trinity and the whole of Creation and beyond. Our true mission is just beginning.

Paul's story

Anxiety and depression dogged Paul's teenage years but Christian friends at university helped him to find someone to look to outside of himself to serve and learn from.

I became a Christian at the age of twenty, when I was an art student at Falmouth College of Arts in Cornwall.

I grew up in south Buckinghamshire, living with my mum and stepfather from the age of eight after my parents divorced and remarried.

I'm not from a religious background at all. The only time I went to church was for Easter and Christmas services as part of a Church of England primary school. I was taken along to Catholic services occasionally by my stepfather when his two children came for the weekend. I was never a naturally religious person. God then changed my life in its deepest sense because he brought me into personal relationship with him.

At secondary school I can't remember hearing the Gospel at any time. I recall one peer who was a professing Christian but I didn't notice anything particularly different about him or discussing spiritual things with him. One of my peers, from a white middle class background, went regularly to a mosque. It was his own choice, but again he was no different. His lifestyle included smoking, girls and playing truant etc.

By the time that I was seventeen and doing A-levels I had developed problems with anxiety and acute self-consciousness. I was very inward-looking, selfish, moody and depressed. I was avoiding school and had a bad experience taking a hallucinogenic drug with school friends. This made my anxiety and introversion worse. Then I had a major motorcycle accident on the way home from school - where I could have easily been killed. God had mercy and it was only my leg that was run over by a van.

My anxiety and depression continued into higher education. I moved away from home to study a degree in Fine Art in Falmouth. Although it was exciting it was also a particularly nerve-racking time. I was soon seeing the student welfare officer regularly about my anxiety and he was very supportive and caring. Looking back, humanistic therapies were a welcome outlet to discuss my problems but they couldn't deal with the root of my problems - sin, self and alienation from God.

The Lord led me straightaway to several people on the same course who were Christians (or at least professed to be). They were part of the Christian Union which had been restarted at college recently.

These friends were very genuine and caring which I really needed in a strange town and in unfamiliar territory. One friend helped me to move into her shared student house.

Another friend was Steve. Steve had converted from Roman Catholicism when he was nineteen; he is now a Christian pastor. Quite often, when discussing various things, he'd end up bringing God's perspective into it which was unusual and annoying sometimes because it felt embarrassing. He seemed a bit of a religious oddball. I realised that talking about God in everyday situations, not just in a Church on Sunday, made me feel uncomfortable and I wished he wouldn't do it; he talked about sin, my sin.

Yet, despite this tension, I was obviously attracted to finding out more. Through our friendship, he told me about the Gospel and invited me to CU meetings and church services. I was fairly interested in listening to all this with an open mind but was comfortable with my position on the fence, an outside observer.

But God worked within me over about a year, convicting / convincing me that the Gospel was true and that I had to make a decision at some time about what I was going to do with Jesus Christ in my life.

Over the Christmas holidays in 1992, back home with my parents, after reading a Christian book about being changed on the inside, I 'phoned Steve and told him that I wanted to sincerely search to know God for myself in my life. He said it was the best Christmas present he could hope for (he told me later that he had been giving up hope on me ever changing).

Looking back now, this reminds me of the importance of patient, persistent, personal evangelism through friendship.

My decision to be a Christian was a bit scary and surprising but also very natural and rational. I was excited yet at peace. God had been drawing me towards him, gently.

I was still confused about the role of Jesus Christ: why did I have to put my faith in Him? It took me a while to understand that Jesus died for my sins so that I could be forgiven and be made right with God and be fit for Heaven, rather than judged in Hell.

When I told my parents my mum was worried when I used the term "born again" Christian and about going to church twice on a Sunday. She was probably thinking, "Who is this Steve whose influence I was under, a cult leader?!"

It's difficult for us sometimes to see for ourselves the changes that God makes in our lives, but my dad and his wife said that becoming a Christian had changed me for the better (even though they didn't want it forced down their throat!)

I was still an anxious person, too self-obsessed and selfish but had someone to look to outside of myself to serve and learn from.

Becoming a Christian doesn't mean conforming to a stereotype; I'm unique in God's sight. In Matthew 11:28-30 Jesus says, "Come to me, all you who labour and are heavy laden, and I will give you rest. Take my yoke upon you and learn from me, for I am gentle and lowly in heart, and you will find rest for your souls. For my yoke is easy and my burden is light."

As a new Christian I tried a large student popular Baptist church but found it too emotional and lacking in solid teaching. I settled on a less immediately attractive but solid evangelical Baptist church.

There were temptations living in a student house with non-Christians. The Lord kept me going by his power and grace as I saw professing Christians backslide and fall away. It is only God's power that has kept me as a Christian.

I was baptised after graduating in 1994 and led to get involved in the youth work of my church. My mum worried that I would never meet someone in a small church down in Falmouth but I met my future wife, Catherine, in that church as we both served God in the youth work.

"But seek first his kingdom and his righteousness, and all these things will be given to you as well."

I now have two lovely boys. Truly God is good to his people.

Pip's story

Pip had a tumour in his bowel but felt like a bystander. A miraculous recovery followed.

In November 2020 I sent off for a bowel screening test. I knew beforehand that all was not well but me being me had ignored it. After a week or so I received a letter that said that I would need further tests. After a further week I received another letter, this time from the hospital, that said that someone would telephone me to discuss further treatment. An appointment was made for me to have a colonoscopy.

During that procedure I could see that all was not well in one part of the bowel so I wasn't surprised when the doctor told me that I had a tumour in the lower section; they removed a section for biopsy at that time. Because of the Covid-19 virus everything was being done via telephone with hospital visits kept to a minimum so it was over the telephone that the diagnosis of bowel cancer was confirmed. A follow-up letter gave me an appointment with a surgeon to discuss further treatment.

When I met the surgeon she explained what had been found and the options for treatment. In many cases the affected part can be removed and the bowel rejoined but in my case this would not be possible as the tumour was too far down and because I am slim. (Normally "slim" means healthy but it's not a good thing in this case.) There was no other surgical option than to remove the whole bowel and leave me with a colostomy bag for the rest of my life.

I then underwent further scans to show the full extent of the tumour and to see if it had spread to any other parts of my body which, praise the Lord, it hadn't. While these tests continued preparations were made for surgery. It seemed as though I was being pushed in this direction. Various appointments were made for blood tests, pre-operative checks and an ECG. An one point I was told that the surgery had been scheduled for the following week. I spoke to a storma nurse about how to use the bags and was sent some to try out and to see what they felt like on my body. A factor that concerned my family greatly was that the infection rate in our local hospital was at its peak at this time and I would need a stay in ITU after the operation which would put me at risk. I had not had a Covid-19 vaccine at this stage. I asked if the surgery could be delayed until this peak had passed but the consultant said that the cancer may spread in that time.

The strange thing with all of this is that I never took it seriously. It was as if it wasn't happening to me and that I was a bystander watching someone else go through it. As far as I am concerned my body is a temple of God's Holy Spirit and nothing else has the right to be there, so I rejected the tumour firmly in Jesus' name. Many years previously I had the experience of God's healing of my broken toes. I had the most incredible experience of Jesus' love and the enormity of the Holy Spirit that changed me and my life forever. I just assumed that this would be the same experience. However, I have been told that God rarely does the same thing twice in exactly the same way. There were plenty of people praying for me at this time, down here in Cornwall and at my sister's church in South Wales.

One day I had an outpatient appointment with the consultant surgeon. I asked if there were any alternatives to surgery. She didn't answer me immediately but she did examine me again. This wasn't the most pleasant of experiences but all throughout I clearly felt God's presence. She told me that radiotherapy and chemotherapy may be an option but she was doubtful. She said that if I did take this option it would make any future surgery more complicated as the radiotherapy would damage the stomach wall and the treatment itself wasn't without serious side effects. Ultimately though the decision was mine so I was given some time to think about it.

When the surgeon telephoned me to see if I had made a decision I was with my daughter who is a nurse so I asked the surgeon to speak to her which she did. I still did not make a decision so the surgeon offered to arrange a meeting with the radiologist to discuss the treatment and I agreed. It seemed that a final decision regarding my choices kept getting delayed which was giving me more time. After another two weeks I saw the consultant again. I was given all the statistics and told about the side effects. She said that a normal course of treatment would include five and a half weeks of radiotherapy along with a chemotherapy tablet and then at least twelve weeks of chemotherapy treatment. Chemotherapy would mean my going to the hospital every three weeks to have an infusion followed by tablets.

With every scan and every consultation I expected to be told that everything was clear and that I wouldn't need any further treatment but that clearly wasn't in our Lord's plan. Therefore I reluctantly agreed to proceed with the treatment. Prior to the treatment I had to attend hospital for a scan where marks were made on my body that allowed the radiologists to direct beams in the right places. Once again at this scan I hoped to be told that I didn't need the treatment as the cancer had all gone but this wasn't the case and the treatment went ahead. However, just before it started I had a call from a consultant to say that new research had shown that a shortened course was more effective. They would use a higher dose of radiotherapy for five weeks and no chemotherapy tablet until the five weeks was over.

I live only a few minutes' walk from the hospital. I felt that even this was part of God's plan when we moved here some twenty-six years earlier. Even though it was a short journey the reduction in the number of times that I had to go was very welcome. When the appointed day came round I arrived for my first session and was surprised to see just how many other patients were also waiting for treatment. It was a Monday and the plan was to have five days' treatment and then have the weekend off. On the Tuesday I was given a list of dates and times. To my surprise it was only five days and not five weeks as I had been told. The following day I asked about the rest of the five weeks. The plan was checked and the five days was confirmed. This was the first surprise and when I shared this everyone said that it must be the Lord and only He could have engineered it.

Two to three weeks later I had a telephone call about the chemotherapy treatment. The side effects were explained to me. Firstly I would be in self-isolation as chemotherapy destroys one's immune system. I would have an extreme sensitivity to cold that meant that the car heater had to be on for the journey home and I would have to wear a scarf over my mouth. I couldn't use the fridge as inhaling the cold could cause breathing difficulties. The procedure itself took several hours of sitting in a chair while the drug infusion filtered into my body. I was sent home with plenty of different tablets including chemotherapy ones to be taken three times a day, anti-sickness, anti-diarrhoea and steroids.

To say that these tablets knocked me for six is something of an understatement. I couldn't eat or drink; I just sat in the living room in an armchair looking out into the garden or with my eyes closed. This was Thursday, a week before Easter. I took the tablets in the evening and again the following morning and evening. I had some gastric side effects that weren't very pleasant. By Saturday morning I was beginning to feel very unwell indeed and in a lot of pain. By the evening the pain was indescribable. It left me almost in tears and crying out to our Lord for help. It made me mindful of how He suffered on the cross and how my pain was insignificant compared to His suffering. The timing of all this just before Easter felt significant to me.

I had been given a card from the hospital that had a number on it that I could ring for urgent advice in the event of an infection. I didn't realise that I could use this number to ask for help so I waited until the Monday morning. I told the hospital that I had stopped taking the medication. The nurse that I spoke to sought advice from the consultant who told me to wait two weeks which was when our next telephone consultation had been scheduled for. I was not to take any further medication. I began to feel better immediately. The pain stopped and I began to eat normally again.

I felt God say that, as a sign of my healing, my weight would not go below thirteen stone. Praise the Lord, it hasn't! During those few days of treatment I had lost half a stone but within a week or so had put it back on. When I received that telephone call I was asked how I felt. I truthfully replied, "One thousand percent." I told her that I felt completely fit and well. I added that many people were praying for me and that I believed that God had healed me. Another scan was arranged for a couple of months' time. One of the side effects of radiotherapy is pain when going to the toilet. Many times that I went I was in excruciating pain and I cried out to the Lord. I didn't realise that the effects would continue after treatment; the pain continued for about a month before easing.

Before the next scan a friend who also loves the Lord agreed with me in prayer that the scan would be clear and that everything would be gone. (Scripture tells us that when two or more people agree on anything in God's name then it will be done. Many years before we had agreed on something else and, quite remarkably, our prayers had been answered.) Prior to our prayers my friend told me that he had shared my story with another friend and that friend felt that he had been given the scripture about the person who was lowered through the roof of the house for Jesus to heal. When the consultant telephoned two weeks after the scan she told me that the tumour had shrunk considerably but had not completely gone. She said that she knew that this was not what I wanted to hear but that there had been a great improvement. She asked me if I wanted to speak to the surgeon with a view to having the remaining tissue surgically removed. I very clearly said, "No thank you." A further scan was arranged for another couple of months' time.

After this next scan the call was altogether different. The consultant said that the scan showed that the tumour had entirely gone. I told her that she was only telling me what I already knew. I thanked her for all that she had done and told her again of my faith and trust in our Lord. The end result was no further scans and no further treatment - just a 'phone call in six to twelve months to check in. Nothing else is necessary. Praise the Lord!

A week later I received a copy of the letter that had been sent to my family doctor. It clearly said in capital letters, NO TUMOUR. The consultant had included details of my strong belief.

For some reason our Lord wanted me to experience that radiotherapy and chemotherapy, but five weeks of radiotherapy became five days and three months of chemotherapy became three days. I was really ill and in a lot of pain but throughout it all I clearly felt that Jesus and his holy angels were with me. My heart goes out to those who are now going through that same treatment and especially those who don't know Jesus and don't have anyone to pray for them.

I have been able to share my healing journey with many people. When someone comments, "You look well," I am able to reply that I am and that I am healed thanks to the power of prayer and our dear Lord Jesus. Not everyone responds but the most important thing about testimony is that no one can deny it. This is real, it happened and that's a fact.

Something I have thought about and that has amazed me is that the penultimate scan showed that the tumour had not completely gone although it was much improved. If this scan had been clear then some may have said that this was due to the treatment. However it was the final scan that was the one that showed it was all completely gone and this had happened without any further treatment so could only be down to prayer and our Heavenly Father, our Lord Jesus and by the healing light of God's Holy Spirit. "By his stripes we are healed."

Right from the start I wanted to tell the doctors about my faith and the number of people praying for me so that, when I was healed, they would know. I think that my healing has surprised them although they don't really say as much. One hospital pharmacist said, "It's a miracle!" and he wasn't the only one to say that. It has also surprised me how my story has been repeated by many others. I pray for all those who have been praying for me to receive a blessing to encourage them in their faith and trust in their walk with the Lord. So many have prayed for me including the police chaplain and many of my son's Christian police colleagues. All have rejoiced in my healing and in what our dearest Lord has done.

One thing that has been evident throughout is our Lord's presence and the unspeakable joys of the Holy Spirit. I well remember coming back home from having had blood taken. As I drove I started singing in tongues and an overwhelming joy filled me. On another occasion I was on the telephone speaking to my sister in Wales when I felt the Holy Spirit well up inside me. Again I started speaking in tongues, much to her amazement. All I could hear was, "Praise the Lord. Thank you Jesus." This also happened on other occasions. An overwhelming joy just fills you and you have to speak out the words the Lord puts in your heart.

One such occasion was a visit to another sister who was in the process of moving home. She asked me to go and see her and to pray with her. This time it felt like a full song in tongues. It wasn't intelligible to us of course but she felt that it sounded Jewish and that if we had been in Israel they would know exactly what I was saying.

I have also felt our Lord give me specific scriptures to read to help and encourage me. These are Psalm 27 and John 9. John 9 tells of a man who was born blind. Jesus' disciples asked who had sinned, the man or his parents? Jesus replied, "Neither, he was born blind so that the glory of God might be seen in his life." Then Jesus took some mud and put it on the man's eyes. He then instructed him to go and wash it off in the pool at Siloam. The scriptures then tell us that the man was healed.

The pool at Siloam holds a special significance for me. In February 2006 on a cold and frosty morning I was in a wood in Devon. It was very early in the day and I had gone there to do some chainsaw assessments. I usually arrived early to unlock the gate and have a drink before the candidates arrived but on this particular day I had a 'phone call to say that the first candidate wasn't coming. This wasn't unusual. I had a couple of hours to wait before the second candidate and I used the time to walk into the woods and spend some moments with the Lord, praising Him for His amazing creation. As I walked up the track into the woods I noticed a small stream flowing down through the trees with a small pool at the bottom. I continued on through the woods and after I time turned round to walk back to my car. When I reached the stream I felt drawn to go over to it. I stood there for a while when I clearly heard, "Go over and wash your hands in the water." It was a very cold February morning but, trying to be obedient, I did so. I remember the water being freezing. However, even more was to come. "Now cup your hands and pour water over your head." Really? On a hot summer's day this may have been welcome but not in frosty February! However, as I am prayerfully obedient to what our dearest Lord tells me to do, I cupped my hands and poured freezing cold water over my head. As I did so the words, "The pool at Siloam" suddenly came to me.

At that time I didn't know where in the Bible that came from and so had to find out. However this is not the end of the story, far from it. The next day I was back to do more assessments but I don't recall it being quite so cold or frosty that day. What shocked me, and still does now when I think about it, is that the stream and the pool were no longer there. You could see where it had been but there was no water there at that time for me to wash my hands or pour over my head. That day I learnt an important lesson: we must do what God asks today for it might not be possible to do it tomorrow.

I was pleased that the consultant put my healing into writing as I am sure that anyone who has experienced a similar blessing will appreciate. It is another way to affirm that Jesus has won the victory. I try to spend an hour with the Lord most mornings, although not always if I'm working. The hour goes by very quickly indeed.

One morning, after I had received that letter, I felt God say that He wanted to teach me about angels. I also want you to read the book, "Angels," by Billy Graham. I wasn't sure what books I had by which authors but I knew that I had some about angels. After a search in my collection I found that exact book. It was very old: the pages had yellowed and the inside cover revealed that it had been lent to me by someone thirty years ago. (My sister has since been in touch with the lender and she doesn't want it back!) I have shared this with two of my sisters and neither appeared to be the least bit surprised. One said that, after I had spoken about angels, everything she then read referred to them. After all, angels are very Biblical and sent by God from heaven to bless us and protect us. Sometime later I clearly felt God say, "I am going to appoint a special personal angel to watch over you." What can you say by way of response except, "Thank you Lord. Praise your holy name"?

I have asked God on numerous occasions what the name of this angel is and never felt an answer. However, on one occasion I just said something like, "Come on Fred," and so that name has stuck! It seems right. If it isn't then I trust that the Lord will tell me so. I feel that the Lord wants me to get to know this special angel and to be aware of his presence. As yet I haven't had this experience but I do believe that more than once, when I have been driving, he has been there to protect and guide me.

With me it is a matter of "work in progress" so who but our dearest Lord knows what will happen today, tomorrow or in the future? We just have to wait and see. Exciting isn't it?

One final point that I must make is that on one occasion, whilst praying, I was asking our Lord what I could do to thank and to praise Him for all that he has done for me when, to my amazement, I very clearly heard him say, "It's not what you can do for Me, rather what I can do through you." That left me speechless and for that matter it still does.

Just after Easter, Wednesday 21st April 2021, about three weeks after stopping the chemo treatment, it was during my morning prayer time that our dearest Lord showed me a very clear picture.

I was standing in a very large courtroom, standing in the dock, facing a judge. He was sitting on a bench overlooking the court. I had no idea what I had been charged with. But as I stood facing him I was aware out of the corner of my right eye, someone standing to my side. They were dressed in a light brown suit. I never did see them properly. Then they spoke. I couldn't hear what they said but after they had spoken the judge said to me, "Case dismissed. I don't find that you have any case to answer." Then the picture vanished. But what a vision! Doesn't it say so much?

Robin's story

"...creator of the rolling spheres, ineffably sublime."

In 1996, aged thirty-three, I was about to get ordained as a priest in the Church of England. Waking up one morning I lay there reflecting on my life's journey in my fifteen years since leaving school. As I looked back it seemed haphazard and higgledy-piggledy, full of wrong turns, cul-de-sacs, at times floundering and not knowing where I was going or how I was getting there. I thought to myself, "Wouldn't it be great to know that God's hand has been upon me, nonetheless, leading and guiding, despite the messiness of the zigzagging, wandering path?" As I ruminated, I pictured in my mind all the places I had lived since birth, seven points on the map of England, including the parish where I was about to move to begin church ministry. As I visualised the locations, I realised that they seemed to form a pattern, like a spiral moving inwards. I got up and immediately took an old road atlas and drew the points of my seven residences then joined the dots. Sure enough, a perfect spiral moving clockwise inwards, without deviation, without overlap of the continuous chronological line starting in strict order from my childhood home to the present and then on to my soon-coming move. "Perhaps," I thought, "this is the answer to my question - that indeed somehow God's providence has been there all along, but only now, with the benefit of hindsight, can I see it."

A couple of weeks later I was on pre-ordination group retreat. One of the hymns featured during our services there was the stirring, "Crown Him with many crowns." My attention was particularly caught by the verse that seems to allude to God as providential cosmic guide through history -

by implication both global and personal: "Crown Him the Lord of years, the Potentate of time, Creator of the rolling spheres, ineffably sublime." The phrase "rolling spheres" brought to mind the wonder of the revelation of my life's geographical spiral, those rolling lines across the map that seemed so definite and precise. Evidence of a divine hand at work or a strange, coincidental anomaly; a lucky chance?

That weekend my ordination service took place in the local cathedral. Afterwards friends and family came back to our new home for refreshments and company. As my sister stepped through the front door she handed me a small card. It is her usual custom to create her own greetings cards, for whatever occasion, with a design or a drawing. I opened the card in front of her and for a moment I stood there speechless, my mouth dropped open in astonishment. She had drawn a simple spiral, with the words running between the lines, "Happy ordination Robin," and the date. She knew nothing of my recent spiral revelation. So I looked at her quizzically and asked, "How come you've drawn a spiral?"

She replied, "Oh, I couldn't think what to do, so I just did anything." I noticed that her spiral went in the same direction as mine on the map of my life's journey - clockwise going inwards. And she had drawn it using coloured crayons, a different colour for each part of the continuous line - the same number of coloured sections as the number of residences on my map. I then told her why her little card was so significant. To this day I keep it in a frame, perhaps my most precious possession.

At the conclusion of my three-year curacy, my trainee posting as a church minister, I was invited by the local bishop to move to a group of village parishes a few miles away - which happened to continue seamlessly the inward journey of the spiral.

A decade later I was on the move again, but this time to a completely different region, and the integrity of the spiral seemed at last to be broken. I felt a little sad about that, but I knew that post-revelation I must seek to rely on God's mysterious hand and not be governed by a spiral as if the shape itself were somehow divine. My new posting was to be in a group of church parishes that took their corporate name from the local river that has its beginnings there. As part of my preparation for the post I bought a large-scale map, carefully drawing on it with a highlighter the parish boundaries, and out of interest the titular river too, its flow and course from its starting point... The river made the shape of a spiral. I realised that, of course, my spiral revelation was not meant literally to be about geography, rather it is a dynamic, like the fingerprint of God - that can manifest itself anywhere, the message being, "You could go anywhere, and my spiral integrity, my fingerprint, my providence and guidance would still be with you - even if you can't see it clearly till years later. One day you will look back and you will see everything. How everything is planned and meant to be."

I find it wonderful to see again and again how spirals reveal their form unerringly and recurrently in the fabric of the universe from the cosmic to the microscopic, and often in the natural inclinations of human artistic design and motif. They always put a smile on my face and a quiet, inner sense of peace and assurance.

God's fingerprints are everywhere.

As I write these words, I do so having just this morning come across divine words given to visionary mystic Julian of Norwich over six hundred years ago (*Revelations of Divine Love*, chapter 11):

See, I Am God.
See, I Am in all things.
See, I accomplish all things.
See, I never withdraw mine hands from anything created,
nor never shall, without end.
See, I lead all things to the end for which I ordained it from
the beginning,
by the same power, wisdom, and love with which I created
it.
How can anything be amiss?

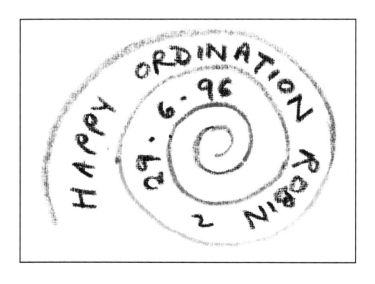

Steve's story

Step by step Steve became more and more taken over by the lure of pornography until God had had enough. After a very painful period that followed he returned to full spiritual and physical health.

As a child I would spend an idle moment leafing through my mum's *Littlewoods* catalogue, mostly for toys and other things that might take my fancy.

As I got older I moved onto a section that I had always previously flicked past. It was the ladies' lingerie. It started to attract me more and not because I was thinking about making a purchase any time soon. Magazines such as *Playboy* and *Penthouse* were literally on the top shelf at newsagents' but it was easy enough to get one's hand on a copy. The dentists wasn't a very rich seam but I used to go to what was considered quite a trendy barbers when I was at school. As I sat and waited to be called most of the men seemed to be reading the car mags. I, on the other hand, pretended that I was reading *Playboy* articles. Those around me thought that it was quite funny.

When I was in the sixth form one of my friends sent off a coupon from the small ads that he had torn out from one of the magazines. A few weeks later he took delivery of a pornographic publication that had been sent in a plain brown envelope from Holland. It was passed around the class and we were allowed to tear out one page each. That kept me going for months. I didn't do much more after that for many years but the seed had been sown.

I got married and had children. I went to work for a bank in London and I'm still there.

Lockdown in 2020 came suddenly and I found myself working from home for the first time ever. My children were out at school during the day as was my wife as a key-worker. Sitting at the dining table with a laptop is okay for the first couple of weeks or so but once the time stretched beyond the equivalent of a summer holiday I began to get very bored in the early afternoon. To relieve the boredom as well as for my own pleasure, I took to looking at a website that featured erotic art, although it was mostly photos. I justified my viewing to my conscience by saying to myself that it won't hurt, just watching a little bit; it's just a little treat for all the work I had been doing in the morning. When I had had enough of that I moved onto something that some may call pornographic but I tried to think of it as just a bit of amusement. From there it was a small step each time to videos and then the videos became worse than pornographic, they became explicit, then obscene and after that I don't even have a word for what I was seeing, I was just pushing myself further and further into a world that I didn't want to inhabit. All my instincts and my conscience said, "No," but I just kept on going. And it was so easy to view. No shops, no hairdressers, just a laptop and a bit of fun at two o'clock every afternoon. I even put an app on my 'phone direct to my favourite site for occasional "top-ups."

I believed in God and occasionally I would say, "Sorry," to him because I knew that he would forgive me but the idea of repentance is that you don't do it again. But I did, on and on and on. "It's only a little thing," I would say to myself. Well it may have been so to start with but having been caught in its grasp I was getting in deeper and deeper to the extent that if anyone had come into the dining room and seen what I was viewing they would have been rightly shocked and horrified, maybe even had me arrested. I had no idea of the damage that was being done to my mind, my body and my soul quite apart from to those whom I was watching. For all I knew they could have been trafficked, abused, enslaved or worse. As for me what I was watching I couldn't undo; it was imprinted in my mind and I was slowly becoming desensitised to what I was seeing. The algorithm just kept pumping more and more extreme material onto my screen. I shudder now at the thought of where it was taking me; I can't think of anything much that I didn't watch and it was affecting my relationship with my innocent wife. I was inadvertently zapping her of any intimacy with me. Why should I bother? I was having fun although each afternoon it was only for a few minutes on the screen but what I was watching was devoid of the one thing that my wife could offer and that was something that is mentioned hundreds of times in the Bible - love.

One afternoon as I sat at my laptop God had had enough. Obviously he didn't bring what happened to me onto me but I had effectively rejected him so where was he? I suddenly had the most excruciating pain in my back. It was so bad I screamed out aloud. I just sat there, stuck on my chair, not daring to move. I was like that for four hours until my younger son returned from school. He gave me a couple of paracetamol and the pain finally started to slowly subside. The following day at exactly the same time I decided that it had been a one-off and I needed to catch up on yesterday's missed "episode." As I typed in the website address the pain returned only this time it was even worse. I didn't think the agony could get any worse but it did. I clicked off the laptop and managed to lie down on the floor.

That is where my son found me, again after four hours. The next day in the afternoon I only had to think about going on the website and the pain returned. This time it was two pains, either side of my back and they both went down a leg, crossing over my groin as they went on their way down to my toes. I was in a bad way.

I tried to go to see a chiropractor but when I got in my car to drive to him I was unable to press on any of the pedals, it was if I had no muscles in my legs, so I went back indoors. My GP came round and got me to lie on the bed. He asked me to raise my legs as far as I could. I couldn't raise them an inch. He said that he would book me a referral with a view to getting an MRI scan. He suggested physiotherapy wouldn't make it any worse and that I should consider going private given the length of a wait to go on the NHS, and off he went.

By now I had totally abandoned my daily "little treat" but every day at around the same time the excruciating pain would return. It also manifested itself at other times of the day also, but mostly after lunch. I managed to get to the hospital for my referral and subsequent scan - I made sure that I went in the morning - and the result eventually came back that I had an inflamed disc but as to how it happened...

The doctor suggested surgery but I had other ideas. I wasn't proud.

One afternoon at around two o'clock I sat on the dining chair and prayed. I said to God that I was sorry for all the wrong that I had been doing, for watching what was distressing to my soul, my mind and those that were probably unwilling participants in the videos. I vowed that I would never, ever watch pornography and worse ever again. That afternoon, for the first time in several months, I had no pain. The pain didn't come that day and it never returned. Slowly the physio helped me to get my legs working again and by the time I had a meeting with the consultant to discuss my surgery I was effectively back to full health.

I have never looked at pornography again and slowly the images that were imprinted on my mind began slowly to disappear, thank God. God allowed me to suffer but when I prayed to him he took that suffering away. I used to drink quite a bit but I've managed to all but stop that also. I feel so happy, happier even than before lockdown and I now voluntarily go into the office nearly every day. I've deleted the app that I downloaded and when I'm now occasionally working from home, at two o'clock I get out my Bible.

Tom's story

Struggling and on antidepressants, Tom managed to make it to a church service then his world changed.

In 2018 I experienced the perfect storm of life events. After leaving university I had fallen into Human Resources and ended up working for a local authority.

I was running redundancy programmes and was also in the process of being made redundant myself. At a sports club that my children were going to there was a serious safeguarding issue. Then there was a death in the family. It tipped me over the edge.

At work, someone asked, "Are you OK?" and I broke down. He said, "I think you should go home," but I thought, "I can't. I've got a meeting to go to." Eventually I went to my doctor.

Admitting to being unwell was the hardest thing I've ever done. When I went in I didn't know what to say. I said, "I'm struggling," and then I just felt tears coming down. The doctor gave me a prescription for antidepressants and I basically spent the next few weeks bedbound.

Around the same time the parents of my daughter's best friend invited us to church. My daughter had been before and my wife had always believed in God. I wasn't against it; I just didn't know either way.

We wanted to go but I was still bedbound so my wife responded to the invitation by saying, "We can't come, but you can come and collect Jessie and take her along."

Somehow, in the five minutes it took them to drive to us, I'd showered, dressed and come downstairs. My wife asked, "What are you doing?" and I replied: "I don't know." I had been in bed for weeks, unable to move. Suddenly I had this motivation to get up.

When I walked into church, a guy looked me in the eye and shook my hand. I felt really strange and thought, "What is that?" Now I would call it unconditional acceptance. With my levels of anxiety through the roof I couldn't understand why I felt comfortable. I kept thinking, "This is really weird. What is going on?"

A few months later I joined a small group. The first session I went to was on anxiety! The first bit of the Bible I ever read was Matthew 6:27: "Who of you by worrying can add a single hour to his life?" I remember thinking, "Why don't they teach this in schools? How have I only just learned this now?"

Going to church put the brakes on my illness. One evening I went to a church service with a friend - he was the first person I had spoken to in months other than my wife - and when we left I was euphoric.

I thought I was fixed. The next day I decided to do all the cooking and cleaning in the house. But by the time everyone came home from work and school I was really ratty. I couldn't understand what was going on and I thought, "I've had enough, I'm going."

I left the house and drove off. I found a car park and just sat there, completely distressed. I felt I was in the darkest place I'd ever been.

At that moment a text came in. It was the friend I had been to church with the night before, thanking me for going with him. In that second, it changed everything.

I felt God reach for me; it was literally like a hand came down and he said, "No, come this way." Soon after that I learned about God leaving the ninety-nine to find the one. I kept thinking, "That's what happened!" I felt like I'd been saved in every interpretation of that word.

While I was bedbound my wife had started to attend the Alpha course. Each week, she would come back and tell me what she had learned.

It felt like fuel to me; I couldn't understand why I was so hungry for this. There were times when she would come back and say, "We were praying for you this evening." I knew something was happening because while she was out I had been lying in bed and had felt a bubbling-up feeling. It was like being cleaned out. So bizarre but incredibly kind and gentle at the same time.

One day my wife bought Nicky Gumbel's, "30 Days: A practical introduction to reading the Bible." One of the readings was the story of the prodigal son.

I identified with the older son because I was holding on to an awful lot of bitterness to the point where I couldn't sleep at night. When I read that story the feelings all fell away. I felt free. That was the start of my healing.

I left my job in July 2021. I didn't know what I was going to do next, but I felt like I was in God's polytunnel. I was like an odd-shaped flower you find at the bottom of the garden. No one knows what it is yet so let's see what happens.

The church taught me to knock on the door, that I'm here for a reason and I've got gifts. This was stuff I hadn't heard before.

My wife was a self-employed business and personal coach and she asked me, "Why don't you join me?" It all seemed natural. Now my wife and I are working on ways to blend faith and good mental health, through training courses and Christian coaching cards.

Over the years, I've lent more into my faith and serving in church, and I haven't had any time off for poor mental health.

That's a miracle in itself. My old boss used to describe me as the guy who sat at his desk and didn't say much. Now I'm like, "Well, if you get me talking about Jesus, I can't shut up."

Tony's story

Career-criminal Tony found himself in the midst of witchcraft in the Peruvian jungle that he had travelled to looking for redemption and a truth to set him free; what he found through taking ayahuasca was a whole lot worse. Eventually he found the Truth and that did set him free.

I was born into a working class family in south London.

For the first ten years of my life everything was great. My father was a builder and my mother a housewife. I have a sister five years younger than me.

Overnight something changed and my parents split up. My mum started to drink a lot and my father left. Then my mum started seeing a guy whom I would call a gangster. I don't particularly like that word but the fact was he was linked with gangs up and down the country. He had money, style, flash cars, that sort of thing. That's when I kind of got catapulted into the start of a long period of crime. Obviously I wasn't doing much at ten years old but I was being sort of groomed by other guys. Some would come to our home packing guns. I would be taken to boxing events and things like that; for me, a young boy, that was all good, that was all fine but the big problem behind it was that this guy was beating my mum and beating her a lot. Now when you've got to get up for school and it's one or two o'clock in the morning and she's bloody and drunk and depressed and even suicidal this is going to have an effect on a young lad and of course it did, both on me and my sister.

Even at that young age I told myself that if this guy ever touched my sister, if he started to bully her, I would have something to say about it even though I was a young child so I grew up in fear. When I reached around twenty-one years of age I was coming out of prison having served some time for house breaking. This guy, who was still with my mum, asked me if I would like to go and work with him. It was something of a love / hate relationship but in some respects I wanted to do it and so I did. Unfortunately, after a short time he did start to bully my sister and, I don't like to brag about it but, he did end up in a bad way and was in intensive care; thankfully he pulled through. However this episode gave me a so-called reputation. I didn't have anywhere else to go because I was still only a young man with a lot to learn; I was full of fear but I was very good at not showing the world that anxiety. The more that I wore these masks the better at it I became which was hiding what was really going on deep down inside of me. I would just push all of these fears down into the basement. At this point I now realised mistakenly that this was the only road that I could take and so I became what you might call a career criminal. I didn't go back to jail anymore but really my whole life was one prison sentence. Every day I suffered with depression. I was by then drinking a lot and taking loads of drugs including cocaine and amphetamines. I was actually living a lie but I had created this person that I had to show the world. There was no way I could really do anything about it as I had gone in so deep. I couldn't change; I just had to keep going.

One relationship after another would be broken; I would just jump from one situation to another. A lot of money went through my hands because of the connections I had made through my younger years. It's not something you could learn in school, I wasn't that good at school; I was preoccupied with all of what was going on in my life.

I left school when I was fifteen years old with no academic qualifications. The only qualifications I had were through being around these other guys, the so-called hard men. I found myself going from one extreme to the other. I just became more and more violent and my life became more of a misery even though I was wanting for nothing. I had what they had - a lot of money, flash cars, plenty of different, nice-looking women, VIP treatment in the clubs and all the trappings of the shiny things of that world. It all may sound very nice but the reality was it was one big lie. Fast forwarding I found myself living this life. This was my life. I reached my early forties and I'm now so depressed and suicidal. Another marriage has just broken down, another relationship was broken, yet another relationship was broken. There were more children and I wasn't fathering them properly. I was getting even more depressed. I was now living in a caravan on the south coast and I was trying to drink myself to death. I was also on the crack cocaine pipe. There had been times in my life before when I've been under Brighton Pier, for instance, with a gun under my chin - a .38 revolver - wanting to end it all at two or three o'clock in the morning, suicidal, out of my brains on cocaine. I was a young twenty-two year old so I'd always suffered with these kinds of mental health issues. I was constantly taking drugs through my life and the only thing that really kept me together, or should I say what I thought kept me together, was because I was into crime and at quite a high level and so I had other people that you had to look out for. This meant that I had to keep my head reasonably together to make sure that I wasn't going to get captured myself or something else bad isn't going to happen to me. I was surrounded by violence.

I then found myself in this caravan all these years later and I had become very, very sick. A friend came to see me - a man I'd known for a long time, and he told me that he wanted to help me. He said that he'd heard about this potion that you can take in Peru with shamans. He said that I would then find healing. So I went out there. I got myself together and within a couple of weeks I'd managed to book a flight and go out to Peru.

Even when I was in that caravan alone I was seeing things. I would call them spirits; they were flying around me and along with the voices that had come into my head I had already gone too far. Taking drugs severely like that can make you go too far; you can press on and push through into dimensions that we just don't understand. I was now in this terrible dark place and I knew I needed spiritual healing. I knew it was a spiritual problem and that it wasn't just the drugs. I had taken drugs all my life; I knew that I'd stepped into something that was almost unreal but it was real, it was very, very real, and I knew that if I had gone to see a doctor they wouldn't understand what was going on. I knew that I had to go to dire extremes. I sorted myself out and I went out to Peru. I flew into a town called Iquitos, a city that is known as the capital of the Peruvian Amazon. I was staying in a small hotel where I got talking to some other westerners. Iquitos is well-known for travellers, especially drug takers and light seekers if you like - people that go there tend to be those who want to know the meaning of life and whether there is anything more than this Earth and what this life has got to offer. They're looking for the truth, they're looking for a truth that will set them free. Part of me was looking for that truth also: a truth that would set me free, that would set me apart from the evil that I'd been involved with - all of the crime and the viciousness that was inside of me, the violence that took place in my life almost from day one or at least from a very young age.

I got talking to these people and I discovered that they were going out the following day to stay with the Shipibo tribe that lived four hours by boat from Iquitos. They were to be spending fifteen days with the tribe. Whilst there they would be taking a potion called ayahuasca which is a hallucinogenic brew. It's psychedelic but the people of this tribe have been taking it for thousands of years. It's traditional to them but if you want to use one word for it, it's witchcraft. I had no idea about any of that and so I decided to go with the group; they had one spare space in a hut where I could stay with them. The next day I got on the boat and off we go for four hours down the Amazon river. When we arrive we're greeted by the Shipibo tribe with whom we're about to spend the next fifteen days in spiritual exploration. So now I'm going to go to realms in order hopefully to come back a better man than I had left behind in England. I was totally giving my life up in every sense, in every way. I knew that I had to go all the way in this as I was already a dead man. I knew I was sick. I had a voice that was in my head that was saying, "This time you've gone too far." It was continually telling me, "This time you've gone too far."

I saw and experienced things that would change me forever.

The first ceremony started and the shamans come into this big circular hut that we're in. We're all sitting down and we're all several metres apart from anyone else. It's approaching midnight. We're wearing white as we were told back in Iquitos that we should only dress in this colour.

There were candles in the centre circle, some people are holding crystals and crystal skulls. It was very New Age. There were plenty of New Age types there, others not so much so but it appeared that everyone was looking for the same thing and that was the meaning of life. Could they go into realms that will give them the answer to their lives and why they exist? There were some there who were suffering from depression, with suicidal thoughts like me, and they wanted healing.

The shamans came in with the witch doctor and they started to pour out this potion, ayahuasca, into eggcup-size jars. Then they came round to give us a jar each. They asked each of us whether we wanted a whole cup or just a half. I had already been advised only to take half a cup because it's so very, very strong and if you wanted you could always have taken another half a cup later on, maybe two or three hours in. On average the brew works for about four to six hours. We all took the potion and after about twenty minutes it started to kick in. I had no idea of the spiritual consequences that I had then landed myself in in trying to get well. I had got myself into a situation that wasn't going to then get me changed for the better for a long, long time. As this thing started to come up on us I closed my eyes. My head was then a mass of kaleidoscope patterns and my mind was going out as I was trying to pull myself back. I noticed this witch doctor was sitting in front of me and he was blowing mapacho smoke over me. Mapacho is like their local jungle tobacco. To this tribe it's a very spiritual kind of product; they use it to cleanse the dormitories, the wooden huts and the ceremony hut before the event takes place. The reason they do this is because they believe that it repels evil spirits and negative energy.

The smokers among us were all smoking mapacho. The shamans were also using Palo Santo which is a dead wood that they burn and then waft around your body in a figure of eight. They also wave it around the door openings, in fact anywhere that they believe they need to in order to repel evil spirits.

Then the ceremony started properly.

The shamans are singing, the witch doctor is also as are the Q'eros which is another grouping that is present when all of a sudden everything went silent. There was always the murmur of the jungle out there. The animals were constantly making a noise but at this moment the noise stopped as did the sound that was coming from the birds. The power that these witch doctors and shamans were commanding in that place was like nothing I'd ever seen or experienced before. The room was completely silent. There was a man to the left of me and he started to make noises and so I looked at him and as I was doing so some grown men started to scream and cry out at what they were hearing. The noises coming out of this man I can only describe as Jurassic-type sounds. He was the closest person to me and he was clicking and groaning. Whatever it was that was in him - this thing, this spirit that we couldn't see at first, it started to attack me as well. I didn't know why but can only assume that it was because of all the darkness that was inside me. I'd lived a life of crime and as an old man said to me once, "Son, no crime goes unpunished," and I knew in that hut on that night, that that meant something. Somehow I was linked and I felt as if I was being punished for all the wrong that I had done in my life. I had been Satan's frontline soldier for a long, long time. Now this thing was attacking me; it was coming down into my throat and I began rolling around being sick and saying, "You're not coming into me; I'm not evil," which was kind of ironic because really if I look back over my life I've done so many things that were wrong and that you would put in the box of evil.

This thing started to get stronger and stronger and I'm now going to call it a demon because that's what it was; this demon, when I looked, I could clearly see it coming out of this man. It was two or three metres higher than his head and as it came out, it was coming out of the man's head, his head dropped down and he had his legs crossed. Then he was silent. As he became silent the demon began making the same noises as the man had been making before moving back down into him. Then the man lifted his head again and started to make the same noises. It was a demon screaming and clicking and just making these terrible sounds through the man; he was completely possessed. There were grown men in that hut screaming, there were women screaming and all the while the shamans were trying to stop people from going away from that hut. They knew that you knew they couldn't let people run into the jungle, they were trying to keep them all in that hut. I didn't try and run away, I was just rolling around. I remember holding my throat trying to stop this demon attacking me but it was coming in and it was making me vomit even more. I wrestled with this thing for hours and hours and hours and it was truly the fight of my life. I had been in many situations that I'm not proud of; I've done plenty of nasty things to people and I'd had some things done to me. I'd had people looking for me with guns, with money on my head. I had people that wanted to kill me and they were going to get paid to do it. I had lived a life, a dangerous life, but what I was experiencing in that hut was in a completely different league. In fact I was out of my league because it was supernatural; it was a demon, it was evil that I was dealing with. My eyes had been opened up to something that I could never ever have imagined existed in this world. I knew of good and evil, we all know that there's good and evil in the world - you only have to open your eyes, but I didn't actually understand that demons are real and that demons manifest themselves; they're in this world that we are living in. This demon opened my eyes at that point. I might have been under this potion but it was the chanting and the witchcraft that was also spoken over this potion that is made over a long time. The witch doctor stirs it in the cauldron and they reduce it over hours and hours throughout that day before we take it in the evening. They say stuff into this brew, they speak curses into this mixture; they might think that they're healing people, they might think that they're doing something good and they're in contact with other worlds. In fact they are but these worlds in my opinion and in my experience - there were other people in that hut that were screaming - these worlds are not there for our for our good; they are hostile worlds.

Somehow I got through that evening.

It was the early hours of the morning. The sun was coming up and people were lying around in the hut. Many were asking, "What was that?" as was I. Nobody would say what it was but they knew - it was an evil spirit. It was a demon, a hostile spirit. At that point I decided that there was no way that I was going to go back into the ceremony hut and do any more of that potion. As that same day wore on I went and spoke to the shamans. One of them was from New Zealand and so obviously he spoke English. I said to him that he should take the man with the demon in him out of the camp and go to this particular tree. We had been to a place in the jungle where there's a tree. It's called "The Sacred Tree" it's probably a thousand years old. It's a great big, wide thing, very old, and they worship it. So in my naivety I said, "You should take that man out to the tree tonight, strap him to it and get that spirit out of him." In my mind I believed that maybe that was possible, that they could take the evil spirit out of that man. They refused, they didn't listen to what I was saying, maybe they knew it couldn't be done, I don't know. What I do know is that they were also out of their league; they couldn't control the evil that had been drummed up in that camp that night so that was enough for me. The next day I said that there's no way I'm going in for any more of the ceremonies (they were once every two days) but my problem was I had nearly two weeks left before the boat would pick us up. I could have taken a canoe as the Indians had canoes that they used to go fishing every night. They would depart about three o'clock in the morning as it was the coolest time of the day. They would fish for piranha which we would eat every day. I could have taken one of their canoes but we were probably forty miles away from Iquitos. There was no way that I was going to try to follow the river on foot. When we had arrived the tribesmen had said to us that when we bathed in the river we needed to make sure that we all bathed together so that we would make a lot of noise. This would hopefully keep the large anaconda snakes that are in the river at bay. So there I was in the middle of the Amazon jungle with no army experience so I wasn't about to go and trek that number of miles. Of course there are all sorts of other things out there as well. The New Zealand guy, who was one of the shamans who had set up the tour with the other people that were there, persuaded me to stay saying, "If you leave they're all going to want to leave." I weighed up the pros and cons and concluded that I was probably better off staying where I was. However I would not be participating anymore.

As the second ceremony day came I was still trying to prevent people from going in and doing more. There was a lot of fear in the camp. Maybe one or two were very eager to get in there and do more but for the most part the people were really just wanting to be as close as possible to the shamans including the New Zealand guy; they were stuck there as I was and they mostly didn't want to make waves. I guess maybe I was a bit more outspoken in some ways. I said that there's no way that I was going to go back into the ceremony hut and do more. Before they started the second ceremony they walked into the hut doing the figure of eight, one of the shamans would blow the Palo Santo over them as they walked across into the main hut. I just sat on my own waiting for it to begin. I was feeling sick even though of course I'd had no more brew. It had been forty-eight hours and there was no way I was putting any more of that in my stomach, into my system. However I started to feel sick and as they started to chant and so on with the ayahuasca kicking in the last the thing that I wanted to hear, what I was really dreading, was the sound of that demon again. I didn't know if it was going to happen or not but I knew that this thing had been in this man; was it something that had come and gone or was it still in him, had it been in him for a long time? I just sat at the end of a table, an old crudely carved table in a kind of communal area where we would all eat together. I was sitting there on my own, about thirty to forty meters away from the main ceremony hut, when all of a sudden it started to manifest itself again. This demon was making the same noises that it had been making two nights before and again I could hear cries and so on from the hut. I was frightened; I've been in a lot of situations in my life but now I felt like I was in hell. I sat there and I put my head in my hands.

I detested the man that I had become. I just didn't know how my life had got so bad, that I was then in the middle of nowhere with this hellish stuff going on around me and I was frightened. With my head in my hands I went back to a default mode.

I hadn't come from any kind of Christian family but what I will tell you now is that I went to Sunday school two or three times as a child. This was only because the leaders would give you chocolate when you left to go home.

I had tears running down my face, frightened to death in the middle of nowhere in the middle of all this witchcraft and then I just said, "God, please help me God, please help me Jesus, please help me." My mind went back to a man I saw on a cross as a young boy and I asked for help. I also asked that he would protect or that God would protect the people that were in that ceremony hut and protect us all from the hell that we were in. At that point I started to feel a degree of protection and of hope so I never moved my hands or my head for all that time all through that night. I just had my head in my hands and I was praying for help and protection. I was still sitting there in the early hours of the morning when the potion was wearing off for the others. One of the shamans came into where I was sitting. He sat down beside me and asked, "Were you praying last night?" I said that I had been. There was no way he could have known anything about what I was doing as they had never come into the hut where I was sitting. He then asked me who I was praying to and I replied, "Jesus." I might even have made the sign of the cross. He looked at me as if he was trying to read my thoughts telepathically. He was simply looking at me whilst he was peeling a banana when he just stood up and walked away. He was stony-faced, like he didn't understand what was going on or that something had messed up their plans. I didn't know what that was at the time. I realised that as the days went on I just had to sit this out. Other people started to join me; there were more people that were coming away from these ceremonies that were held once every two days. I asked the guy that had the demon, "Where do you think this is coming from, how has this come about, and why is this happening to you? What's this thing in you?" He confided in me, "I've come here to try to get free because I've been involved with sorcery and spiritualism, that kind of thing. I felt something enter me one night. There was a man in my front room and we had crystals and skulls. I felt something enter me and I knew it was something nasty so I've come here to try to get set free." I knew then that in a way I was there trying to look for the same thing. I was looking to be delivered out of darkness and to be set free.

I carried on every two nights. I would put my head in my hands and I would just pray. I would pray for help and I would pray for protection. I managed to get through those two weeks and finally the boat turned up to pick us up after this time. I was so grateful when it arrived in the creek as I wanted to get out of there like you wouldn't believe. I wanted to get back to Iquitos and I did; I wanted to get back to a place where there was some kind of normality whatever that meant. I just knew that I wanted to be well away from the camp and all of the evil that had been going on in there. Of course we had made friends whilst we had been at the camp. We had gone through a lot of stuff together. We knew each other by name and some had drawn together closer than others but no one spoke about what any of us had experienced in the jungle. It became like a bit of a taboo subject really. The whole thing was shelved and not one of us attempted to speak about it.

When we arrived back at Iquitos we returned to the hotel. Some people had rooms booked there and some were leaving straight away to fly home on that same day. I said goodbye to everyone and went up to my room. The next morning I wanted to get up early and leave. Some of them were going to Machu Picchu where they were going to be drinking San Pedro which is another kind of potion, up in the mountains. However I wasn't looking for another new drug as I was there to get healed so I departed. I told them that I wished them well but I didn't want any more to do with that kind of thing so the next day I flew to the capital Lima and then on to Cusco where I spent a few weeks. It was during my time in that city that I realised that I was coming under a tremendous spiritual attack. It was as if I had put my head through some kind of spiritual membrane. I was in a hostile place. I would close my eyes at night and there were these reptilian eyes that were looking back at me.

I then started to drink a lot once more whilst I was still in Cusco. I was knocking myself out with their local brew and whisky and so on. After I had been there a few weeks I flew back to London. When I arrived back things were just getting worse and worse instead of getting better. I realised that nothing good had came out of taking this potion ayahuasca. I had been taken to realms that I could never have known existed. These realms were hostile; the depression was still there. I didn't feel anything had left me from that area of my life and I was now drinking as much as

I had before I left. I was being held down at night when I was sleeping; it felt like I was being suffocated and being poked under my ribs. I felt a fingernail being drawn across the top of my head. I woke up one night and to my left I saw this child. It looked about six or seven years of age. It had big black eyes that were just staring at me and not blinking. It had black hair that was swept back and maybe it was kneeling. It was just looking at me and waiting for me to make a move or something. I turned and looked up at the ceiling and I pleaded, "God please help me." I looked back and this thing was still staring at me. Then, in my fear, because it was a demon and it was there to torment my fear because it was evil, it put its right hand up once I had cried out to God. It put its right hand up and it giggled like an innocent little child would giggle behind its hand. It giggled at my fear. It wasn't giggling for any fun, it was giggling at my torment and fear. Then I looked and it looked away and then I looked again and it had disappeared. This went on for only six or seven seconds but I was looking at a demon in front of me, making expressions towards me and not going anywhere and then putting its hand up. At that point I knew that I was at the point of suicide again. I had come full circle. I had been to Peru and returned and now things were a hundred times worse than before when I was in that caravan on my own on the south coast of England. I was at the point of taking my own life.

I was lying one night again on my own on a sofa and again the usual thing would happen. I would open and close my eyes repeatedly. At that time I was taking diazepam as well to try and help me sleep, to try to knock myself out but I didn't have any medication this particular night. I lay there and as usual being terrorized and then I just closed my eyes. The reptilian eyes were there and these other faces were coming in. It was almost as if a hole had been opened up in my mind, like a third eye that had been opened up, and this evil stuff was coming in through the third eye. I simply closed my eyes then opened them again. I was at the point where I just wanted to give up and as I closed my eyes again I was given a vision of a man in low down position, low to me on my right side. In my side view of him he was a slim man. He had a prominent nose and a very short, cropped but very curly dark beard and he also had dark curly hair. It wasn't all the way down to the shoulders, it was collar length. He was wearing something like a cream-coloured tunic.

He was wearing a crown of thorns.

His mouth was moving and it went on moving for a few seconds, maybe three or four, maybe five seconds and then, "pop," he disappeared. All of a sudden the faces, those evil faces that were coming in at me disappeared as well. So as I opened my eyes, continually closing then opening again, checking what had gone on I realised that those evil faces had gone. When I had them closed it was black like it should be so that person that represented the crown of thorns, that vision represented the Son of God and he was praying for me! He was speaking, he was saying something to these evil beings and as a consequence they left. First they left and then he left. I remember lying there in the early hours in the morning on the sofa with cushions behind my head and I once more had tears running from both of my eyes down the sides of my face. I remember hearing them drop, plop, plop, onto the cushions. I don't know why I've remembered that so much but I smiled and just said, "Thank you. Thank you for helping me." I managed to get to sleep and I slept peacefully that night.

The next day I knew that that vision represented the Son of God, that it represented Jesus Christ with the crown of thorns. I knew that his words were more powerful than the things that were attacking me and had been doing so for nearly three years by then. I knew that there was something good, that there was a good god, a good presence, a good force that was at work trying to help me and trying to kill part of me in some way and protect me from the evil that was coming at me and had been doing so for a long time, in fact had been for all my life. I realised that I wanted to get closer to this person, to this god and I knew that the only way I could do it was to start looking into who Jesus was, who the Son of God was because of this vision. I knew that there had been some kind of healing that had taken place, that he had turned up and helped me. So at that point I started to look for Christian ways of being healed. I got baptised but I was still doing stuff that I shouldn't have been doing.

As I started to look a little bit deeper I found a Christian healing and deliverance ministry. One day someone randomly gave my mum a card and told her, "You need to give that to somebody." It was for a Christian healing ministry. I knew that God was showing me that I needed deeper deliverance. I realised that as I listened and watched and read what they were talking about that they were dealing with really heavy situations: demon situations and heavy spiritual situations. I knew that I was tangled up in something and I needed help and so I walked into that healing and deliverance ministry. I spent nine days there, at Ellel Ministries. It was there that I was taught about what repentance meant and what it meant was to turn around and to look at Jesus Christ, to look at God, to look at him and say, "I am agreeing with what you want to do for me which is help me because I know you want to help me. Right now I know you want to help me. You've revealed yourself to me and I know there are demons and I know there's a devil and I know these things have been attacking me for so long but I know that you're helping me and I know that your word that's written in the Bible says that you want to do just that." And once I understood this through being taught about it over nine days I then got on my knees on the grounds of that healing and deliverance ministry. There's a wooden cross there, on the ground, and I said, "Please help me Jesus; please forgive me; please set me free from all of the evil that's attacking me. I repent, I turn around, I look at you and I'm sorry for all of the evil that I've done." At that point I surrendered my spirit, my heart and my life to him because I knew that it was the only choice I had left. He was the only avenue I had left. I was gone. I was being spiritually attacked continually and had been for three years and at that point I surrendered.

The next day, that was on a Friday, the next day on the Saturday they had a thing that was called Jesus Heals Day. It was Biblical teaching where people would come in from outside. They would hear some teaching and then they would receive some counselling and prayer into their individual situations with two people, two individual ministers, sitting in a big hall. Two to three hundred people came in and I went down there, to the hall, and I sat there and I listened a bit to some more teaching. At the end of that teaching they invited people to come up and receive prayer and counselling. I stood in the queue in the middle and as I started to walk closer I began to really tremble inside and I felt fear. I was so hot. My legs were like jelly. There was something going on, there was a fight going on inside of me but I just managed to keep moving forward. I knew what I needed at that point and it was deliverance. I needed to be delivered from evil and I was agreeing through God's word with what he wanted to do for me which was to set me free, to set the captive free, that's what he was promising to do. I was allocated my two ministers; they were two men. I sat down on the third chair and I was sitting in front of them. One of them asked, "What is it that you want prayer for today Tony? What do you need deliverance from?" Straightaway I just started to say, "I want to be forgiven of the witchcraft that I've been involved with in the jungle as I understand this is a tremendous thing that's opened me up to evil and I need help to be set free from it and I want Jesus to help me. I want to just repent of that in front of you two men okay?" In the Bible I had been taught that when we confess our sins to one another and pray for one another we receive healing and so I was bringing it into the light. These two men of God were witnessing that I was bringing it, I was spilling the beans. I was saying in front of two witnesses, "God, I'm sorry for all this." At that point, as I was repenting and saying sorry and asking God to forgive me, asking Jesus Christ to forgive me, one of the men started to pray and then the other man started to pray over me. They had a hand each towards me and they started to pray in a way that's called praying in tongues which I didn't understand too much about at that point but it's the Holy Spirit, the spirit of God speaking through these men. At that point and it was only just a minute, maybe two at most, I'd sat there - it was that quick because I'd agreed with what Jesus was doing and wanted to do for me and his word was aligning with his truth - all of a sudden I felt something coiled in the bottom of my spine. It went up the back of my spine and my diaphragm. I sort of made a grunting noise and my head went slightly forward as I felt three or four coils come out of my neck: one, two, three and so on. I jolted and I felt something like a snake leave me. Suddenly I had clarity. My temperature went back to normal. I wasn't sweating any more. I was sitting there and everything just felt clear straightaway. I knew that something had just been expelled from me and the way that that happened was because I'd agreed with God's word and had asked Jesus to forgive me. He had the power to deliver me and the Holy Spirit, the spirit of God, was more powerful than the demon that was inside of me, therefore it had to leave when it was told to leave because I was asking Jesus to help me and I was saying sorry. I stood up and I said thank you to these two men.

I walked out of that hall and I knew that my life would never ever be the same again after that day.

The spirit that left me was without doubt a serpent spirit. I realised that going back to the jungle, that the spirit that the Shipibo tribe and other tribes worship is the spirit of the anaconda. My mind then went back straightaway to the ceremony hut and the tapestries that were all around the hut. They were sewn together, created and sewn by the women. Each separate tapestry was a different scene but the anaconda, the snake that they worship, was always in each one somewhere. I then knew for sure that the moment that the anaconda serpent had been ejected from me it went back to the witchcraft that I had been involved with and the spirit that I had been under. I had allowed it to enter me because I had agreed with what they were doing. I had come under that spirit and under the authority of the witchcraft, of the witch doctors and the shamans that allowed full access for that spirit, I had allowed that demon serpent spirit to then enter me. The Bible calls it Leviathan although you don't need to think of names - it was a serpent

161

demon spirit, so once I had repented of the witchcraft and the jungle and taking the potions, it was at that point that I agreed with the authority that God's got through his son Jesus Christ or Jesus has over me, he had the authority and the power anyway but I'd agreed with him, and at that point the Holy Spirit said, "Right you've got to leave," and straightaway I was delivered and I knew that the Holy Spirit is more powerful than any other spirit in the universe. I didn't even know if I could get well I was that far gone. I didn't know if I was ever going to get well again but the Bible says that God so loved the world that he sent his one and only son that whoever believes in him will not perish but will receive eternal life. God showed me, Jesus showed me that day how much he loves me and how much he loves humanity and how much he just wants us to agree with him so that he can heal us and set us free.

Therefore my life now looks like this: I went back to this deliverance and healing ministry because my life had been a mess from day one. I spent three months living there. It was then that I started to understand more about the Bible. From that period of my life, that was 2017, I've read and studied the Bible every day. I now know that the word of God is true; it represents his will for us, it's his road map for us to follow, to keep us out of the trouble that I got myself into.

I understood after receiving more healing how I could then help others get out of bad situations that they have been involved with, people that have lived lives where there are certain curses on their lives.

To bring this back to the beginning because I want to link this back to what I know is true. My grandparents were involved with occult practices which means basically witchcraft. They were involved with things that were against the will of God, looking for illegitimate knowledge in heaven, in spiritual realms. They were using tarot cards, palm reading and an Ouija board. I remember as a young child of five years of age, my earliest memory was of staying at my grandparents' house and a vicar coming to the house. They had invited him to visit because there were things going on in the house, things flying off the windowsill. I remember seeing and sensing stuff in the hallway of their home but I couldn't understand it or explain it because I was only a child of five. The vicar came in and he was walking around with the Bible. The reason they'd invited him was because of the stuff that was going on but when he left they had failed to tell him that they were both involved with witchcraft, with the occult; they were inviting demons into their lives. The Bible says, God says to us that you shall have no other gods before me, not one. It also goes on to say in that same piece of scripture that those curses will go down to the third and fourth generation because when we go against God's word we come away from his truth and we're not under any godly covering. As my grandparents were involved with witchcraft and inviting demons to come from demonic realms into their lives and into my mother's life and my life, it would have carried on down to my children, to the third and fourth generation. It's written, the Bible says, "It is written." Whenever it's written it is written by God and that's the truth of the universe and so I've broken all of the laws of the universe, well not all of them maybe but most of them. My grandparents and their parents before them had broken the laws of God and these effects were now being shown in me. I believe one hundred percent now that I serve God and I do plenty of prayer ministry and counselling people, that after several years'

Bible study and praying with people that have got serious spiritual problems, that this nearly always goes back to problems that involve people who have done things in their generations before them and have been involved with ungodly situations, inviting and looking for illegitimate knowledge. They've gone into realms that they didn't understand even if it was for fun; they've invited the demonic into their lives and then they start to feel that their house is unlucky or our lives are unlucky or there's poverty in our lives or there's always illness or there's anger and crime and violence and addiction. There are so many different things, a constant breaking down of relationships like in my life - one to another, never being able to find what they're searching for, being tormented in a way that you don't understand. You know it's there but you don't understand where it came from. We might call it bad luck, we might feel like we've always wanted to get on in life and do well but we've never actually been able to do so. It's as if there's something invisible holding us back. All of these things are spiritual problems so when we sit down with a Bible and we agree with what God says and we agree with what Jesus has done for us which is to stand in our place, God loves us so he stood in our place, and he said, "I'll pay the price, it's finished." Jesus Christ said on the cross, he cried out, "Tetelestai!", it's the Greek word for, "It is finished," or it can be translated as, "Paid in full." That means that all of our spiritual debts that we've piled up through being against and away from God's word, away from his will, doing it on our own, when we come back to God's will, come back to his word and we agree with him, Jesus says, "It is finished!" He stood in front of you before God, God came and manifested himself for inhumanity and he stands before God the Father and before us and he says, "It is finished!"

164

Tony

What do we need to do? We simply need to walk through the cross, walk through the cross and say, "Yes. I surrender my life. My life has been wrong. I'm suffering with addictions, I'm suffering with anger issues, betrayal, nothing works out for me. I feel like there's a poverty on my life. I can't ever move forward, it's like my life is full of bad luck. I feel like I'm being victimized all the time even though I mean well." All of these things are generated from curses that come on our lives because of generational sins that have happened before us and of course we then walk into these situations and we sin the same way as our ancestry has sinned because of the devil that's behind this network. What he's trying to do, what the Bible says, is that he comes to steal, kill and destroy. He wants you to do the same as your ancestry so that the curses carry on past you to the third and fourth generations. He wants to steal your soul, he wants to kill and steal and destroy you and your family, your children and your children's children, but...

God came to give you life and give it abundantly. God did that by sending his son. God the Son, Jesus, came and sacrificed himself for his creation which is you and me. On the cross he cried out to tell us, "Paid in full!" You can't do it on your own, I couldn't do it on my own, but when you come into agreement with Jesus Christ you're coming into the will of God and the sacrifice he made for us.

If you know God is calling you, don't delay because it's a gift. Salvation is a miracle.

Now what?

First and foremost, the time is now. If you want to invite Jesus into your life and to live in eternity with him, and you haven't already done so, this prayer is for you:

"Lord Jesus, I believe you are the Son of God who died to pay the penalty for my sins. I open the door of my heart and ask you to be my Saviour and Lord. I ask your forgiveness for all my sins. Please forgive my sins and help me to live for you."

Now tell someone! If you have no one to tell, tell me! You can email me at johnhemmingclark@gmail.com or give me a call, anytime, on (UK) 07968 525692. If I'm not available leave a message and I will get back to you. Or write to me at the address on the copyright page.

If you're not ready to say that prayer, read on.

The thing is, the encounters that ordinary people have had with Jesus that are in this book are not unusual. It's just that they're sometimes hard to find but they're out there. Step into any church and there you will find those who are or have been on similar journeys. Some, in fact many, conversions may not be as dramatic as a few of those that you have just read - it seems to me that, to rephrase the famous saying, the lower they fall the harder they climb - but everyone, including you, can receive the peace that the world cannot give.

Maybe you're apathetic towards God. The bad news for you is that there is no place for apathy with Him. Don't shrug your shoulders and say, "Whatever." The time is now. And the choice is yours.

Agnosticism, that is to say, "Maybe he does exist, maybe he doesn't," isn't an option. It's either he does or he doesn't. There is no middle way. C S Lewis put it this way, in *Mere Christianity*,

"I am trying here to prevent anyone saying the really foolish thing that people often say about Him: I'm ready to accept Jesus as a great moral teacher, but I don't accept his claim to be God. That is the one thing we must not say. A man who was merely a man and said the sort of things Jesus said would not be a great moral teacher. He would either be a lunatic - on the level with the man who says he is a poached egg - or else he would be the Devil of Hell. You must make your choice. Either this man was, and is, the Son of God, or else a madman or something worse. You can shut him up for a fool, you can spit at him and kill him as a demon or you can fall at his feet and call him Lord and God, but let us not come with any patronizing nonsense about his being a great human teacher. He has not left that open to us. He did not intend to."

If you simply don't believe remember that atheism is itself a belief system. You have chosen not to believe and you will need to then explain the reason for the world, life, us, space, eternity, infinity, order, emotions, thought, speech and how all these things came about by accident and not design. It's a very dark road to go down but there is light. You may not believe in Him but He believes in you. He died for you, He rose for you, He lives for you and He loves you. Don't allow it to remain a one-way street.

Lastly, if you are trying to believe but are finding it difficult to take a leap of faith then simply pray, "Lord, if you're real make yourself real to me; speak to me."

167

If you want to contact me or any of the contributors to this book then get in touch. Don't just put this book down without taking a conscious decision to do so. Your life depends on it.

And if you do decide to put it down, don't do so before you've read it again. God is speaking to you now. Listen to Him.

Acknowledgments and further information

The stories
Thank you to those who have contributed their first-hand experiences to this book in their own words. If you would like to contact any of the individuals please contact me using the details in the previous section and I will forward your message. Some of the contributors' details, and further information, can be found below.

Amy's story
Amy (not her real name), is a families' & children lead worker in a church.

Bernard's story
Bernard is Pastor Bernard Suwa.

Charmaine's story
Charmaine is Charmaine Joshua.

Ernie's story
Ernie is Ernie Matthews. He died on 20th July 2015 at the age of 84. His testimony is included in this book in remembrance of his great service to the church he attended in Stony Stratford for many years as a deacon.

Helen's story
Helen is Helen Shapiro. Her singles "Don't Treat Me Like a Child," "You Don't Know," "Walking Back to Happiness" and "Tell Me What He Said" sent her soaring to international stardom at the tender age of fourteen, and has been going strong ever since 1961! Until recently Helen devoted herself solely to her Gospel Outreaches, having come out of show business at the end of 2002, after forty-

two years of touring. Currently she ministers as part of the Messianic trio called HEBRON. Helen is married to actor John Judd and they live in Greater London. Her website is www.mannamusic.co.uk

Jim's story
Jim is Jim Payne. He lives in Chislehurst, Kent and is a retired motorbike racing champion.

John's story
John is Rev John Draycott, a recently retired Anglican priest.

Kevin's story
Kevin is Kevin Cockburn. Read more of his remarkable story in his excellent book,
"The Tattooed Saint: Born into a Cult."
ISBN: 9781838483852

Laura's story
Laura is Laura Maxwell. She writes,

You can find many of my interviews on my YouTube channel   www.youtube.com/@LauraMaxwellExSpiritist including but not limited to:
    Eddie Bennett
    Dana Emanuel
    Jeff Harshbarger
    Former Hindus
    Rev. Mark Hunnemann
    S A Tower
    Other former alien contactees and UFO researchers, Guy Malone of Roswell, New Mexico and Joseph G Jordan include multiple similar testimonies from

former UFO enthusiasts and alien abductee survivors in their books, see below. Joseph and I interviewed each other on our respective programmes, available on YouTube.

My work is shared worldwide, not just through Christian but also secular and New Age TV, radio, books, schoolbooks, magazines and so on. Many of those have been translated into other languages.

My website: https://ourspiritualquest.com

Recommended Reading
To read similar testimonies I also recommend the following books, or articles and interviews with these Christian authors online.

Seeing Ghosts Through God's Eyes: A worldview analysis of earthbound spirits by Rev. Mark Hunnemann

The Kingdom of the Occult by Walter Martin, Jill Martin Rische, and Kurt Van Gorden

Former New Ager:
Inside the New Age Nightmare by Randall N. Baer

Former Spiritualist Mediums:
Enticed by the Light: The terrifying story of one woman's encounter with the New Age by Sharon Beekmann

The Beautiful Side of Evil by Johanna Michaelsen

Former Paranormal Investigator:
Ghost Hunter Spooked by the Real Supernatural: Dana Emmanuel's story by Ian White, page 5, October 2020 issue. (This newspaper article can also be read online at goodnews-paper.org.uk)

Former Alien Contactees and UFO Researchers:
> Piercing The Cosmic Veil: You shall not be afraid of the terror by night by Joseph G Jordan and Jason Dezember
>
> Come Sail Away: UFO phenomenon & the Bible by Guy Malone

Former Wiccan:
> From The Craft To Christ: The allure of witchcraft and the church's response by S A Tower

Former Witch:
> A Soul For Sale: A true story by Carol Kornacki

Former Meditation and Yoga Tutor:
> In Search of the True Light by Mike Shreve

Former Satanist:
> Dancing with the Devil: An honest look into the occult from former followers by Jeff Harshbarger. (This book includes my longer testimony.)

Liam's story
Liam is Liam Husband and he is Minister of Hope Community Church in Bournemouth.

Lisa's story
Lisa is Rev Canon Lisa Battye and she is a Team Vicar in Didsbury, Manchester.

"Man Alive!" is written as a detective story on the subject of the Resurrection of Jesus Christ. Using Sherlock Holmes' methods of dissection and evidence, Michael Green gives a well-constructed argument in favour of the truth of the Resurrection and its meaning for Christianity.

Mandy's story
Mandy lives in Chislehurst, Kent and is a mother to two children.

Marion's story

Marion is Marion Morgan. She was received into the Roman Catholic Church in 1969 and has since been involved in ecumenism at local and national levels, parish work, freelance writing and caring for an autistic adult. For the past ten years she has been a member of the Order of Consecrated Virgins.

Following his death, Marion is no longer a carer but lives quietly with her dog, adapting to a new way of life. She is still involved in St Mary-on-the-Quay parish in Bristol and turned 80 in 2022.

Paul's story

Paul is artist Paul Ayers.

Pip's story

Pip is Pip Richards. He was baptised Samuel, his father's, grandfather's and great grandfather's name, going way back. He got the nickname as a toddler and it stuck. His first son is Samuel as is his son.

Pip joined his father in landscape gardening but specialised in tree surgery in Surrey. He moved to Truro in Cornwall in 1973 at the age of twenty-six living with his sister and her husband and their three children for four and half years until he married the love of his life, Stephanie, with whom he had three children, Louisa, Sam and Joe. In 1984 Pip dropped a chainsaw on his foot and broke two toes giving him intense pain. His much older sister, Mary, who would later become an ordained Anglican priest and was to a certain extent involved in the healing ministry, visited and prayed with Pip. The pain disappeared and Pip felt bathed in a wonderful warmth and healing light - he experienced the wonderful power of God's presence. Throughout Pip's life he repeatedly said the two most important things were breaking two toes and meeting and marrying Stephanie. In the 1980s there was a global recession and his tree surgery work dried up. He found himself Head Gardener on the Trellowarren Estate near Helston, part of which was the Trellowarren Christian Fellowship of which he became a part. At one time he offered himself for ordination and attended a residential selection committee but was not accepted. He was an enthusiastic deeply committed Christian man, believing and practising fasting. He was quite a character.

Pip died in 2023.

Robin's story
Robin is Rev Robin Stapleford, based at Colkirk in the Upper Wensum Benefice in the Church of England, just south of Fakenham.

Tom's story
Tom is Tom Stevens. He is a business and personal coach and co-founder of WYN@LIFE Coaching. www.wynlifecoaching.co.uk

Alpha course: Alpha is an 11-week course that creates a space, online or in person, where people are excited to bring their friends for a conversation about faith, life and God. www.alpha.org

Tony's story
Tony is Tony Maisey.

Tony writes,

"If you've been impacted by my story and you can draw parallels with any of the content that I've written about then please contact me via my website www.tonymaisey.com. You can email me personally and I'll speak to you personally regarding anything that you may be struggling

with spiritually or if you want Biblical guidance into any anything I've written about. Maybe it's something separate but if it's a spiritual problem then you can find me at tony@insidewarministries.org.
I have written a book on my experiences which is called "INSIDE WAR. From the Jungle to the Jordan." It is available through my website, Amazon or any other of the platforms. God bless you. Tony"
Read much more of Tony's story in the excellent, "INSIDE WAR From the Jungle to the Jordan."
ISBN: 9781610362665
Extracts used with permission from Bridge Logos, Inc. Newberry, FL 32669, USA

"For I do not seek to understand in order to believe, but I believe in order to understand. For I believe this: unless I believe, I will not understand."
St Anselm of Canterbury

"Where is he then, I haven't seen him?"
"You haven't looked!"
South London street, September 1971

Do you have a transformative testimony? Write and let me know at johnhemmingclark@gmail.com
www.johnhemmingclark.com/transformativetestimonies